INSIGHT GUIDES

LISBON

POCKET GUIDE

⊙ Walking Eye App

YOUR FREE EBOOK AVAILABLE THROUGH THE WALKING EYE APP

Your guide now includes a free eBook to your chosen destination,
for the same great price as before. Simply download the Walking Eye
App from the App Store or Google Play to access your free eBook.

HOW THE WALKING EYE APP WORKS

Through the Walking Eye App, you can purchase a range of eBooks and destination
content. However, when you buy this book, you can download the corresponding
eBook for free. Just see below in the grey panel where to find your free content and
then scan the QR code at the bottom of this page.

Destinations: Download essential destination
content featuring recommended sights and
attractions, restaurants, hotels and an A–Z of
practical information, all available for purchase.

Ships: Interested in ship reviews? Find
independent reviews of river and ocean ships
in this section, all available for purchase.

eBooks: You can download your free
accompanying digital version of this guide
here. You will also find a whole range of other
eBooks, all available for purchase.

Free access to travel-related blog articles
about different destinations, updated on a
daily basis.

HOW THE EBOOKS WORK

The eBooks are provided in EPUB file format. Please note that you will need an eBook reader installed on your device to open the file. Many devices come with this as standard, but you may still need to install one manually from Google Play.

The eBook content is identical to the content in the printed guide.

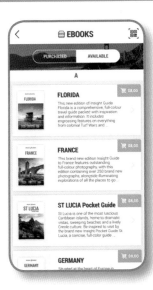

HOW TO DOWNLOAD THE WALKING EYE APP

1. Download the Walking Eye App from the App Store or Google Play.
2. Open the app and select the scanning function from the main menu.
3. Scan the QR code on this page – you will then be asked a security question to verify ownership of the book.
4. Once this has been verified, you will see your eBook in the purchased ebook section, where you will be able to download it.

Other destination apps and eBooks are available for purchase separately or are free with the purchase of the Insight Guide book.

TOP 10 ATTRACTIONS

THE MUSEUM OF ART, ARCHITECTURE AND TECHNOLOGY
MAAT is the newest landmark of the transformed Belem riverside. See page 49.

ELEVADOR DE SANTA JUSTA
A century-old iron lift with great city views. See page 39.

THE TORRE DE BELÉM
This fine example of Manueline architecture guards the entrance to Lisbon. See page 55.

MOSTEIRO DOS JERÓNIMOS
A jewel from Portugal's Golden Age. See page 51.

CASTELO DE SÃO JORGE
Built by the Moors, this castle is where present-day Portugal began. See page 33.

Lisboa
PARQUE DAS NAÇÕES
The highlight here is the state-of-the-art aquarium. See page 60.

MUSEU NACIONAL DE ARTE ANTIGA
Home to the city's finest art collection. See page 46.

THE BAIRRO ALTO
Bars, clubs and restaurants make the 'Upper City' Lisbon's centre of nightlife. See page 42.

THE MUSEU GULBENKIAN
A superb and wide-ranging art collection. See page 57.

THE ALFAMA DISTRICT
Narrow alleyways and red-roofed houses give a taste of medieval Lisbon. See page 28.

A PERFECT DAY

9.00am

Start the day

Breakfast of coffee and pastries at a laid-back café in Alfama, Lisbon's steeply inclined, characterful Mooris district that is topped by the Castelo de São Jorge. Then slowly saunter around the corner to Lisbon's cathedral. The Sé is a handsome, defensive-looking place of worship dating from the 12th century, and forms a contrast to the web of narrow Alfama lanes.

11.00am

Castle views

From here it's a picturesque meander through alleys splashed with vibrantly colourful *azulejos* (tiles), up the steep incline to the Castelo de São Jorge, with sweeping panoramic views over the city and the River Tagus.

2.30pm

Tram ride

Take a trip on Lisbon's most picturesque tram ride, No. 28, and head down to the Baixa district, an appealing grid of old-fashioned streets. Have a wander around the Praça do Comércio, whose proud colonnades overlook the Tagus, before taking a bus westwards along the waterfront to Belém, Lisbon's monumental district.

1.00pm

Lunch

Time for a lazy lunch of grilled sardines or *bacalhau* (salted cod). In one of the family-run restaurants in the backstreets of Alfama.

3.30pm

Belém

Visit the fantastical Mosteiro dos Jerónimos, a frenzy of elaborate carving that's somehow otherworldly in its magnificence, and the Torre de Belém, nearby, Lisbon's classic landmark.

IN **LISBON**

8.00pm

Dinner in Alfama
Dine at Chapitô á Mesa in Alfama (see page 106), perched just below Castelo de São Jorge. The dining room is wrapped by windows on all sides and the lights of the city sparkle below. It's a fantastic way to top off a perfect day in Lisbon.

5.00pm

Custard tarts
Follow these curious sights in Belém with one of Lisbon's finest *pastéis* (custard tarts). Pastéis de Belém (see page 110), which sells well over 10,000 *pastéis* a day, is just the place to sample these delicious, warm-from-the-oven confections of delight. Head back to your hotel to relax and perhaps have an *aperitivo* before heading out again for dinner in Alfama.

11.30pm

On the town
By this time the bar scene at Bairro Alto is just getting going. If you are ready to party, head back into town to see the bar-lined streets take on a carnival, street party vibe. Bar hop until you drop, or head off to Lux (see page 89), Lisbon's finest club, on the waterfront. You can party on from here and watch the dawn of a new day from the terrace.

10.00pm

Fado experience
To experience traditional Portuguese soul music, try a tiny, out-of-the-way place nearby in Alfama, where locals are not averse to giving their all in rendering Portugal's songs of life and loss.

CONTENTS

⬤ INTRODUCTION 10

🏛 A BRIEF HISTORY 15

🏛 WHERE TO GO 27

Alfama 28
Miradouros 29, Alfama gems 30, São Vicente de Fora and the
Panteão Nacional 32, The castle 33, The cathedral 34, A detour
east: two museums 36

Baixa (lower city) 37
Rossio 39

Bairro Alto (upper city) 42
São Roque and Carmo churches 43, Chiado and São Bento
Palace 45

Lapa 46

Belém 48
MAAT 49, Mosteiro dos Jerónimos 50, Monastery museums 53,
Berardo's museum and the discoveries monument 54,
Torre de Belém 55

North Lisbon 55
Museu Gulbenkian 57, Aqueduto das Águas Livres 59

Parque das Nações 60

Across the Tagus 63

Excursions from Lisbon 64
Queluz 64, Sintra 66, Mafra and Ericeira 71, Estoril Coast 73,
South of Lisbon 77

😊 WHAT TO DO 83

Shopping 83
Entertainment 87
Sports 91
Children's activities 93

🍽 EATING OUT 96

🅾 A–Z TRAVEL TIPS 112

🅱 RECOMMENDED HOTELS 135

🌐 INDEX 142

🔘 FEATURES

Lisboa Card 12
Inês and Pedro 16
Azulejos 20
Historical landmarks 25
St Vincent of Lisbon 31
Manueline architecture 51
Calouste Gulbenkian 56
Sintra's country market 69
Fado 88
Calendar of events 95
Port and Madeira 104

INTRODUCTION

Lying with its back to Spain and its face to the Atlantic Ocean, Europe's most westerly country is about three-quarters the size of England. Around 2.9 million of its 10.3 million inhabitants live in Lisbon, the capital, which sits halfway down the coast on the estuary of the River Tagus (Tejo in Portuguese). The city is built over a number of hills on the right bank, facing south, at the estuary's narrowest point, where it shrinks to around 3km (2 miles). The largest bridges in Europe reach across to the expansive delta on the far side.

LAID-BACK CAPITAL

Lisbon's great days are over, its colonies gone. Fortunes have risen and fallen dramatically over the course of its 3,000-year history. Even in recent times, a burst of economic activity that was sparked by the EU at the end of the 20th century is a distant memory, as Portugal struggled to overcome the fallout of the 2008 crisis and the subsequent austerity measures under the EU bailout. Fortunately, since 2014, the country has seen a steady recovery.

Lisbon may have corners that are cutting edge, in its nightlife, designer boutiques and galleries and chic restaurants, but it is also a place that resonates with the difficult-to-define Portuguese characteristic of *saudade* (nostalgia), enjoying a slightly regretful, drawn-out retirement from its time as centre of empire and greatness.

Even when tourists began to arrive in any number, in

A global language

There are 260 million Portuguese speakers in the world, making it the sixth most-spoken language in the world.

the 20th century, Lisbon was seen as a lovely but laid-back provincial capital, known more for the charms of the narrow Moorish-style streets, the beauty of its hand-painted ceramic tiles and occasional ornate architectural flourishes than for economic dynamism. With its neighbourhoods clustered on the sides of hills along the placid Tagus, there are gentle reminders everywhere of Lisbon's distant past: the Phoenician profile of the modern fishing boats; the Moorish expertise with painted tiles; the pained notes of *fado*'s longing and lament.

A tram ride through steep, narrow streets

STREETS AND VIEWPOINTS

The narrow whitewashed streets of the old Moorish neighbourhood, Alfama, twist and turn; they remain the heart of a modest, working-class, inner-city village. Here and elsewhere, *Lisboetas* decorate their balconies with flowerpots, their walls with colourful tiles, and the pavements with mosaics. Building and restoration work is everywhere in evidence, but it is a slow and expensive business and there is a lot to do.

Local women carry bags of bread and groceries up and down Lisbon's hills without complaint, but visitors may prefer to opt for one of the charming century-old electric trams that still trundle through the city, or let one of the eccentric yellow funiculars take the strain. Wandering is rewarded with picturesque nooks or brilliant panoramic views of the city's red-tiled rooftops stepped down towards the river. Whether from one of the lookouts in Alfama, the gardens of Castelo de São Jorge (St George's Castle) or the top of Santa Justa, the iron lift that used to transport workers and residents from the Baixa (lower) to the Bairro Alto (upper neighbourhood), *Lisboetas* never miss an opportunity to take in the whole of their city in its sun-kissed splendour.

Although the cold Atlantic lies only a few kilometres downriver, Lisbon feels decidedly Mediterranean. A sheltered, south-facing location; mild winters allow palm trees and bird-of-paradise flowers to flourish, and the balmy weather encourages an unhurried pace. Despite the inescapable presence of a greater past, this is a modern, cosmopolitan capital, which has a sense of the world outside. The city's streets teem with people of diverse ethnicity and dress. Many are immigrants from Portugal's former African colonies – Angola, Cape Verde, Mozambique – or from Brazil, Macau and Goa, who arrived in Lisbon and soon founded their own little colonies, speaking a slightly softer version of the language and adding spice to the cuisine.

⊘ LISBOA CARD

Lisbon's tourist offices offer a discount Lisboa Card that entitles holders to free Metro (subway), bus, tram and lift transport; free entry into 28 museums and monuments; and discounts of between 10 and 50 percent in other places of interest, as well as discounts in some shops. The card (available for one, two or three days) covers nearly everything of interest to visitors, including sights outside Lisbon, such as the palaces in Sintra and Queluz.

Street scene in Baixa

UPPER AND LOWER DISTRICTS

For the visitor, one of the high points, literally and figuratively, is St George's Castle, perched on top of Lisbon's loftiest hill. From its ramparts, the castle overlooks Lisbon's oldest and most pictur-esque neighbourhood, Alfama. This working-class quarter, once home to the city's elite, survived the tremendous earthquake of 1755 (see page 19), and retains the labyrinthine layout of the Moors, as well as a remarkable village-like atmosphere.

To the west is the residential suburb of Belém, the city's most monumental district. It proclaims Portugal's Golden Age of Discovery with the finest Manueline monuments.

Between the two is the Baixa – 'lower', downtown Lisbon, a com-mercial waterfront district of neoclassical buildings, the old stock exchange and government ministries, quaint shops and grand squares. Most of the Baixa was lost to the natural disaster, an earth-quake in 1755, but was quickly and elegantly rebuilt on a grid pattern.

In the Parque das Nações

The upper city, the Bairro Alto, is reached by tram, lift or steep climb. One of Lisbon's quintessential neighbourhoods, it is home to much of the city's nightlife, including *fado* houses, restaurants and bars. Within the upper city is the chic district of Chiado. Though much of it was razed in 1988 by a devastating fire, it has been impeccably rebuilt. Renovation work that began in the late 20th century has turned the city once again towards the river and the sea. The transport infrastructure continues to be improved. Old quays and warehouses have been transformed into trendy restaurants and hot nightspots, and the Parque das Nações has added interest to the north of the city.

AROUND THE CITY

Monuments to former splendours and cutting-edge museums are not the end of the capital's charms. Lisbon is surrounded by some of Portugal's most appealing spots. To the northwest, Sintra is a magical place, with palaces and *quintas* (estates) studding beautiful pine-clad hills with views of the coast. To the west are the sparkling beach resorts of the Estoril Coast, while over the Tagus to the south are the wild Serra da Arrábida and the fishing town of Sesimbra. Closer to the capital, the handsome Versailles-style palace at Queluz is another major draw for visitors.

A BRIEF HISTORY

Though a legend claims Odysseus as Lisbon's founding father, most hard-headed historians date the city's origins to around 1200BC, with the establishment of a Phoenician trading station. Its name then was Alis Ubbo or Olisipo.

People had settled in the area thousands of years before, attracted to its location on a calm river close to the Atlantic Ocean. Around 700BC, Celtic tribes moved into northern and central Portugal, while the coastal settlements were incorporated into the empire of Carthage.

Recorded history of the city begins in 205BC, when the Romans ousted the Carthaginians and created the province of Lusitania, though not without fierce resistance from the Celts. Olisipo was proclaimed a municipality and later renamed Felicitas Julia – the Joy of Julius – by Julius Caesar. The Romans built roads, cultivated grapes, wheat and olives, and bequeathed the foundations of the Portuguese language. As the power of Rome declined, most of the Iberian peninsula was overrun by tribes from north of the Pyrenees. Lisbon fell at the beginning of the 5th century AD, after which successive migratory tribes controlled the city until the 6th century, when the Visigoths brought a period of peace.

THE MOORISH CONQUEST

In 711, 79 years after the death of the Prophet Mohammed, a great Muslim invasion fleet from North Africa crossed the Strait of Gibraltar, and in just a few years the Moors had conquered most of Iberia. Lisbon became a thriving outpost under Muslim rule. Its castle, begun by the Visigoths, was enlarged, and beneath it, stretching down to the river, the narrow streets of Alfama were infused with an Arabic flavour that remains to this day.

Christians had maintained a precarious foothold in northern Portugal, and it was not until 1139, when Dom Afonso Henriques declared himself the first king of Portugal, that their struggle to gain power met with some success, defeating the Moors at the Battle of Ourique. In 1147 the king recruited a volunteer force from thousands of Flemish, Norman, German and English crusaders on their way to the Holy Land, persuading them to strike a blow against the Moors in return for whatever booty Lisbon had to offer. The successful siege of Lisbon lasted four months. A century later the reconquest of Portugal was complete and Afonso III (1248–79) chose Lisbon as his capital.

THE GOLDEN AGE

In a decisive battle, fought in 1385 at Aljubarrota (100km/62 miles north of Lisbon), João of Avis, recently proclaimed João I of Portugal, secured independence from Spain. A new alliance with England was sealed in the 1386 Treaty of Windsor, outlining true and eternal friendship. A year later King João

⊘ INÊS AND PEDRO

Inês de Castro and Pedro the Just are two tragic figures who could have served as the models for Shakespeare's Romeo and Juliet. Pedro, heir to the throne, defied his family and lived for a decade with the Spanish beauty, one of his queen's ladies-in-waiting. In 1355, three noblemen slit Inês's throat – a political assassination ordered by Prince Pedro's own father, Afonso IV. When he became king just two years later, Pedro exhumed her body, crowned it, and ordered all the nobles to kneel and kiss the skeleton's hand. Pedro and Inês are entombed together in the monastery at Alcobaça.

Henry the Navigator

married Philippa of Lancaster, the daughter of John of Gaunt. Their third surviving son, Henrique, Duke of Viseu, Master of the Order of Christ, became 'Henry the Navigator', who redrew the map of the world.

Prince Henry won his spurs in 1415 at the age of 21, when he sailed from Lisbon in a daring expedition to capture the North African stronghold of Ceuta. It was his first and last act of bravado, for he then retired to the 'end of the world', the Sagres peninsula in the Algarve, where he established a centre of research that gathered together astronomers, cartographers and other scientists whose work magnified the skills of mariners. Their expeditions redefined European understanding of the world. During Henry's lifetime, Portuguese caravels sailed far beyond the westernmost point of Africa. With the colonisation of the Atlantic islands of Madeira and the Azores, the foundations of the future Portuguese empire were laid.

The king who ruled over Portugal's Golden Age of Exploration – and exploitation – was Manuel I, 'The Fortunate', who reigned from 1495 to 1521. Discoveries made during this period made him one of Europe's richest rulers. During his reign the Tower of Belém and the impressive Jerónimos Monastery were built in the 'Manueline' architectural style that eased Portugal from the Gothic into the Renaissance. Whimsically flamboyant and decorative, it is rife with references to the sea.

The most significant expedition under Manuel's flag was Vasco da Gama's sea voyage from Lisbon in the summer of 1497. Rounding what is now known as the Cape of Good Hope, Vasco da Gama found what Columbus had been looking for but missed the sea route to the spices of the East. Reaching Calicut in southern India the following year, Portugal put an end to the Venetian monopoly of the Eastern spice trade by assuming control of the Indian Ocean and attracting merchants from all over Europe to Lisbon. Further territories were discovered in 1500, when the Portuguese explorer Pedro Álvares Cabral reached Brazil.

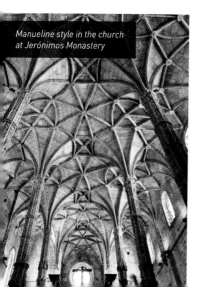

Manueline style in the church at Jerónimos Monastery

TIMES OF TRIAL

When Manuel died, in 1521, he was succeeded by his son, João the Pious. With one eye on the ungodly ways of prosperous Lisbon and the other on the Inquisition in Spain, João invited the Jesuits to cross the border into Portugal.

Although the Inquisition in Portugal was never as powerful as it was in Spain, it persecuted 'New Christians' – Jews who were all forced to embrace Christianity, including Spanish Jews who had been promised refuge in Portugal. Despite these witch-hunts, an outbreak of plague and such natural calamities as earthquakes, by the end of the 16th century Lisbon had an estimated population of 100,000.

When Dom Henrique died leaving no heir in 1580, Philip II of Spain marched in and forced the union of the two crowns. It took 60 years for the local forces to organise a successful uprising against the occupation. On 1 December 1640 – celebrated as Portugal's Restoration Day – Spanish rule was finally overthrown, and the Duke of Bragança was crowned João IV in a joyful ceremony in Lisbon's huge riverfront square, the Terreiro do Paço, known today as the Praça do Comércio.

His grandson, João V, enjoyed a long and glittering reign, from 1706 to 1750. As money poured in from gold discovered in Brazil, the king squandered it on lavish monuments and buildings. His greatest extravagance was the palace and monastery at Mafra, 40km (25 miles) northwest of the capital.

DESTRUCTION AND REBUILDING

The great divide between Portugal's early history and modern times falls around the middle of the 18th century when, on All Saints' Day, 1 November 1755, as the crowds packed the churches to honour the dead, Lisbon was devastated by one of the worst earthquakes ever recorded. Churches crumbled, the waters of the Tagus heaved into a tidal wave and fires spread throughout the city. The triple disaster is estimated to have killed between 15,000 and 60,000. Reminders of the nightmare

are still found across Lisbon; the most evocative is the shell of the Carmelite church in the Bairro Alto district behind the Elevador de Santa Justa, which has been open to the sky since the morning its roof fell in.

Routine problems of state were beyond the talents of the ineffectual José I (1750–77), who could not be expected to cope with the challenge of post-quake recovery. The task of rebuilding fell to the power behind the throne – a tough, ambitious and tyrannical minister, Sebastião José de Carvalho e Melo, later Count of Oeiras, but best remembered as the Marquês de Pombal. Taking advantage of the power vacuum once the earth had stopped shaking, he mobilised all of Portugal's resources for the clean-up. Survivors were fed and housed, corpses disposed of, ruins cleared and an ambitious project for a newly structured city laid out.

Today, the modern sections of the capital are aptly referred to as 'Pombaline Lisbon'. Pombal's achievements are commemorated with his heroic statue, on top of a column at the north end of the Avenida da Liberdade in downtown Lisbon, a central road hub referred to as 'Pombal'. A huge equestrian statue of José holds the main place of honour in the Praça do

⊙ AZULEJOS

Azulejos, the hand-painted, glazed ceramic tiles omnipresent in Lisbon, are not merely decorative. After the Great Earthquake and fires devastated much of Lisbon and the surrounding area in the 18th century, these tiles were widely used to protect buildings from going up in flames again. The name *azulejo* is thought to be derived from *al-zuleiq*, Arabic for small polished stone. At the Museu Nacional do Azulejo you can see how they are made.

Tile panel at Miradouro de Santa Luzia, showing Lisbon's royal palace before the earthquake

Comércio, where the riverside royal palace had been before the earthquake. The king had a close brush with death in an assassination attempt in 1758, after which Pombal inaugurated a reign of terror, with widespread repression.

PENINSULAR WAR AND CIVIL WAR

At the beginning of the 19th century, Napoleon managed to drag Portugal into the heat of Europe's conflicts. The situation became so perilous that the royal family fled to Brazil on board British ships. Taking no chances, they remained there until 1821, 10 years after the crisis was over.

In 1807 Napoleon had tried to pressure Portugal into abandoning its traditional loyalty to England. Lisbon attempted to stay neutral, but when it refused to declare war on Britain, the French army under General Andoche Junot marched in, setting up headquarters in the Queluz Palace, just outside Lisbon.

Statue of Pedro IV in the Rossio

Military miscalculations in the face of a British expedition sent Junot's army packing in 1808. Over the next few years, repeat engagements became notable victories for the combined Portuguese-British forces, largely thanks to the strategic brilliance of the great British commander, Sir Arthur Wellesley (later the Duke of Wellington). After the textbook battle of the Lines of Torres Vedras, north of Lisbon, the French began a long retreat, sacking and looting as they went. Their last outpost in Portugal was evacuated in 1811.

Peace was still to prove elusive, and 17 years later the country was again at war – this time pitting brother against brother. On the death of João VI, his eldest son, Pedro IV, who had become emperor of a newly independent Brazil, fought to wrest the crown of Portugal from his absolutist brother, Miguel I. Pedro won, though he died of consumption only months later, in September 1834, aged 36. His adolescent daughter, Maria da Glória, assumed the throne. She married the German nobleman Ferdinand of Saxe-Coburg-Gotha, who built for her the astonishing Pena Palace above Sintra and fathered her five sons and six daughters. Maria II died in childbirth at the age of 34.

Premature and tragic deaths claimed many Portuguese royals, but in all the country's history only one king was assassinated. On 1 February 1908, as the royal family was riding in an open carriage past the Terreiro do Paço, an assassin's bullet felled Carlos I. A few seconds later another conspirator fatally shot Carlos's son and heir, Prince Luís Felipe. A third bullet hit the young prince Manuel in the arm. Thus wounded and haunted, Manuel II began a brief two-year reign as Portugal's last king. He was deposed on 5 October 1910 in a republican uprising supported by certain elements of the armed forces. The royal yacht spirited him to Gibraltar and later to England, where he lived in exile.

REPUBLIC TO DICTATORSHIP

The republican form of government was as unstable as it was unfamiliar. Resignations, coups and assassinations kept an unhappy merry-go-round of presidents and prime ministers whirling. The nation could ill afford a war, but German threats to its African territories pushed Portugal towards World War I on the side of the Allies.

The war's toll hastened the end of Portugal's unsuccessful attempt at democracy. After a revolution in 1926, General António Óscar Carmona assumed control, and two years later entrusted the economy to António de Oliveira Salazar, then an economics professor at Coimbra University. The exhausted Portuguese finances rallied soon afterwards. In 1932 Salazar was named prime minister. His tough, authoritarian regime – the Estado Novo (New State) – favoured economic progress and nationalism. He kept Portugal neutral in World War II, but permitted the Allies to use the Azores as a base.

THE CARNATION REVOLUTION

When Salazar suffered a stroke in 1968, power was handed to Dr Marcelo Caetano. However, in 1974 the armed forces, discontented by hopeless colonial wars, overthrew the dictatorship

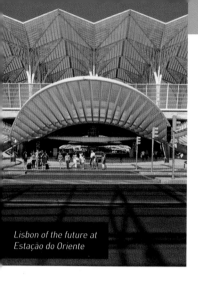

Lisbon of the future at Estação do Oriente

in the so-called Carnation Revolution. Portugal disengaged itself from Mozambique and Angola, and managed to absorb the million or so refugees who fled to a motherland most had never seen. The nation suffered several years of political confusion and great hardship before adjusting to democracy.

With entry into the European Union in 1986, development quickened, and Portugal soon had one of Europe's fastest-growing economies. As host of World Expo in 1998, Lisbon launched a gleaming new neighbourhood, Parque das Nações, east of the city. That year also saw the writer José Saramago win the Nobel Prize for Literature. In 2004 Portugal hosted the European Football Championship, for which new stadiums were built and others renovated.

But the economy began to stagnate and the 2008 financial crisis left Portugal with a budget deficit that was fast spiralling out of control. In 2011, it became the third EU country after Greece and Ireland to ask for a financial bail-out from the EU. It wasn't until 2014, after harsh austerity measures had been implemented and the budget deficit reduced, that Portugal exited the bailout programme. Recent years saw the gradual elimination of austerity measures by the socialist-led government, currently headed by António Costa, and a steady economic revival as well as a decrease in unemployment.

HISTORICAL LANDMARKS

c.1200BC Phoenicians establish Alis Ubbo or Olisipo trading post.

c.700BC Celtic tribes arrive.

205Bc Romans create Lusitania; Olisipo is made a municipality.

5th century AD After the decline of Rome, Visigoths settle in Lisbon.

711 Moors arrive on the peninsula and swiftly conquer it.

883 Northern Portugal (Portucale) regained by Christian forces.

1139 Dom Afonso Henríques declares himself first king of Portugal.

1255 Capital of Portugal transferred from Coimbra to Lisbon.

1386 Treaty of Windsor confirms England–Portugal alliance.

1415 Explorers reach Madeira, starting the Age of Discoveries.

1498 Vasco da Gama opens a sea route to India.

1500 Pedro Álvares Cabral reaches Brazil.

1580 Portugal falls under Spanish rule for 60 years.

1755 The Great Earthquake devastates Lisbon.

1807 Napoleonic troops invade Portugal at the start of the Peninsular War; royal family leaves for Brazil.

1828–34 Civil war between Pedro IV and Miguel I.

1908 Carlos I and Prince Luís Felipe assassinated.

1916 Germany declares war on Portugal.

1932 António de Oliveira Salazar becomes prime minister.

1974 The Carnation Revolution restores democracy; Portugal pulls out of African colonies and a million expatriates return.

1986 Portugal joins the European Union.

2001 The euro replaces the escudo as the national currency.

2004 Lisbon hosts the European Football Championship (Euro).

2007 Portuguese vote to legalise abortion.

2011 Portuguese negotiate an economic bailout from the EU, harsh austerity measures are introduced.

2014 End of the EU/IMF bailout programme, beginning of economic recovery.

2016 Social democrat Marcelo Rebelo de Sousa becomes president, Portuguese national football team wins Euro 2016 in France.

2017 Wildfires ravage vast swathes of Portugal killing over 100 people.

Padrão dos Descobrimentos

WHERE TO GO

Lisbon's waterfront is an arc stretching nearly 32km (20 miles) along the River Tagus. At the western end is Belém and at the eastern extreme is the Parque das Nações, the site of Expo 98. A city map shows that many of the top attractions in Lisbon are within walking distance of the river, but because of the hills and the way in which the sights are spread out, it isn't always very easy to go directly from one to another.

As in many cities, it's best to organise your time and interests according to neighbourhood. The Belém district on the west side of the city holds several of the star visitor attractions, but the central areas, such as Alfama and the Bairro Alto either side of the Baixa, are better for dining, shopping and lingering.

You can travel cheaply and efficiently from place to place by public transport. Buses are quick and straightforward; antique trams ply routes around the old town; and funiculars make light work of steep hills. Lisbon's Metro system is modern and fast, but serves a limited area, though expansion is underway. Taxis are plentiful and fairly inexpensive. Parking is usually difficult or even impossible on weekdays, so a car is best saved for out-of-town excursions.

On arrival, a guided city tour, whether by bus or ferry along the river, can be a good way to grasp the general layout (see page 122).

The Tagus

The River Tagus (Tejo) is 940km (585 miles) long, rising in Spain (where it is known as the Rio Tajo), and passing through Toledo. Its delta, to the south of Lisbon, is an important wildlife area.

ALFAMA

Alfama is Lisbon's oldest, most picturesque and most fascinating area. Here, in a labyrinth of steep, crooked streets, alleys and stairways – a layout left by Moorish occupants of the city – little seems to have changed since the Middle Ages. The whole area between the castle and the waterfront is a jumble of tilting houses with peeling paint, laundry hanging from windows, bars and fish stalls. The streets are so narrow that it's not uncommon to overhear elderly women sharing gossip across balconies.

You are almost certain to get lost, but in this area – safe and easy-going by day – that's part of the attraction. Stick to the narrow streets; if you find yourself in a street wide enough for two cars to pass, then you have strayed from the Alfama area.

A good start to your explorations is at the bottom of the hill at the **Museu do Fado** ❶ (Fado Museum; www.museudofado. pt; Tue–Sun 10am–6pm) in Largo do Chafariz de Dentro. This sets the tone for the soul of the district, with a history of the city's famous music in song sheets, film clips and recordings, and a complete mocked-up *fado* tavern where you can sit and listen to Amália Rodrigues and other bygone stars, then select a souvenir from the CDs on sale.

Nearby is the **Museu do Teatro Romano** (Roman Theatre Museum; Rua de São Mamede, 3 A; www. museudelisboa.pt; Tue–Sun 10am–6pm; free Sun after 1pm), the contemporary

Trams to Alfama

Taking a tram is the best way to get up into Alfama: No. 12 goes from Praça da Figueira and No. 28 from Bairro Alto. They share the same tracks in Alfama and you won't get lost if you follow their iron rails.

Miradouro de Santa Luzia

home of a ruined Roman theatre that was buried in the 1755 earthquake and excavated in 1964.

MIRADOUROS

Alternatively, take the easier path into Alfama, with a tram to one of its vantage points, and let gravity lead you back down towards the river. The **Miradouro de Santa Luzia ❷** is one such bluff on the edge of Alfama. From a pretty balcony covered with painted tiles and bougainvillea there are stunning views over a jumble of tiled roofs that cascade down to the river. Tourists mix with old men in black berets playing cards and chatting. Two detailed and dramatic azulejos (tile panels) on the wall facing the belvedere show Lisbon's waterfront as it was before the Great Earthquake and, in bloodthirsty detail, the rout of the Moors from the castle.

Just up the street is another terrific *miradouro* (lookout point), with even more expansive views. A small café on **Largo das Portas**

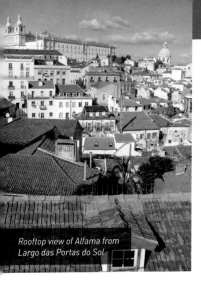

Rooftop view of Alfama from Largo das Portas do Sol

do Sol serves snacks and beverages; visitors have been known to remain here for hours on end.

Between the two, and just above the Miradouro de Santa Luzia, the fine 17th-century **Azurara Palace** has been filled with magnificent pieces of furniture, Chinese porcelain, a priceless silver collection, and several tapestries from 16th- to 19th-century Portugal and its colonies, forming the **Museu de Artes Decorativas** (Decorative Arts Museum; www.fress.pt; Wed–Mon 10am–5pm). The museum belongs to the Ricardo do Espírito Santo Silva Foundation, which was established in the 1950s by the eponymous banker and displays his valuable collection. The Foundation has 18 workshops where artisans practice traditional crafts such as woodwork, metalwork, gilding and bookbinding.

ALFAMA GEMS

Some of Alfama's lesser-known attractions are best stumbled across by accident, through an arch or around a blind corner. Here is a selection of them.

Rua de São João da Praça is where the first king of Portugal, Dom Afonso Henriques, entered Lisbon through the Moorish defensive wall on 25 October 1147. The remains of a tower that was part of the Moorish defences can be found on **Largo de São Rafael**.

Rua de São Pedro is Alfama's boisterous main shopping street and site of a fish market. On weekday mornings, it's a cacophony of shouting fishmongers, gossiping shoppers, chickens, dogs and children playing football.

Igreja de São Miguel (St Michael's Church) was built in the 12th century and restored after the earthquake; it has a glorious ceiling of Brazilian jacaranda wood and a rococo gilt altar screen. To the east, **Igreja de Santo Estêvão** (St Stephen's Church) has a 13th-century octagonal floor plan, but has been rebuilt several times over the years; the over-hanging back of the church nearly collides with the front gate of an old palace.

The alley called **Beco da Cardosa**, with its blind-alley off-shoots, is the very essence of Alfama's appeal. On **Beco do Carneiro** (Sheep Alley), ancient houses sag towards each other across a stepped-street barely wide enough for two people; above, the eaves of the buildings actually touch.

⊘ ST VINCENT OF LISBON

The remains of St Vincent are kept in a beautiful silver reliquary at São Vicente de Fora. Vincent was martyred at Valencia in 336, but when the Moors took that city in the 8th century the inhabitants fled by sea, taking the relics of St Vincent with them. They were driven ashore on the coast of Algarve at the cape now known as Cape St Vincent, and there the relics remained until Dom Afonso Henriques had them brought to the capital and deposited in the church he had just built. Two ravens faithfully escorted the saintly relics, which explains why many a Lisbon lamp-post bears the symbol of a sailing ship with a bird fore and aft.

SÃO VICENTE DE FORA AND THE PANTEÃO NACIONAL

Just beyond the dense quarters of the Alfama, but linked to the neighbourhood, are two of its top sights. Though you might have trouble navigating the crooked streets up to it, the twin towers of the **Igreja e Mosteiro de São Vicente de Fora ❸** (Church and Monastery of St Vincent Beyond the Walls), rising above a hillside east of the São Jorge castle, are impossible to miss. Founded by Dom Afonso Henriques immediately after retaking the city from the Moors (tombs of the Teutonic knights who helped him lie beneath the Sacristy), it was reconstructed in the 16th century around the time of the Inquisition. This huge Italianate building succeeds in combining substance with grace. The entrance to the **monastery** (Mon–Sun 10am–6pm) is on the right, where there is a pleasant café.

Built over an enormous cistern, many of the monastery's walls and courtyards are lined with *azulejos*, though the *Fables* of La Fontaine, depicted in 38 *azulejo* tableaux, have been removed and repositioned for display on the first floor. An exhibition explains the history of the Patriarchate of Lisbon, granted by the Pope in 1720, and pantheons contain tombs of the patriarchs and of Bragança royalty, including Catherine of Bragança, queen of Charles II of England, and Carlos I and his heir Prince Luís Felipe, assassinated together in 1908.

Thieves' Market

Behind São Vicente, around the Mercado Santa Clara, Alfama's colourful *Feira da Ladra* (Thieves' Market) is held every Tuesday and Saturday from dawn to dusk.

A further pantheon, the **Panteão Nacional ❹** (Igreja de Santa Engrácia; www.panteaonacional.gov.pt Tue–Sun 10am–5pm) is the other dominant building in the area, just downhill from the monastery. This grandiosely domed marble church was begun in the 17th century, but the final touch, the cupola, wasn't completed until 1966. To describe something as the 'works of Santa Engrácia' is to call it an endless task.

Santa Engrácia remained a church until a few years ago, when it was deconsecrated and became the national pantheon, honouring great figures in Portuguese history with symbolic tombs in the sumptuous rotunda. To one

The Castelo de São Jorge

side are the real tombs of presidents of the republic and contributors to Portuguese culture, including the famous *fado* singer Amália Rodrigues (1920–99), which always has fresh flowers. You can climb to the gallery for a view onto the marble floor of the rotunda, and to the terrace and dome, though there is often a queue for the lift.

THE CASTLE

Almost every hill in this elevated part of town has a *miradouro*, but the best panorama of all belongs to the **Castelo de São Jorge** ❺ (St George's Castle; www.castelodesaojorge.pt; daily 9am–6pm, in summer until 9, camera obscura 10am–5.20pm), which is reached by the steep alley and steps that continue up from the tram stop on Rua de Santa Justa. From the ramparts, you can look out across the centre of Lisbon, over the Baixa to the Bairro Alto, down to the river and the Ponte 25 de Abril, as far as Belém.

The facade of Sé Patriarcal

The Moors, who ruled Portugal between the 8th and 12th centuries, clung hard to their castle but were finally dislodged in 1147. The new proprietor, Dom Afonso Henriques, expanded the fortifications, but earthquakes as well as general wear and tear over the following centuries left little intact. Restoration has since given new life to the old ruins, even if that means that much of the castle is not original.

Apart from the sensational vistas and the chance to roam the battlements, the castle is worth a visit for the park gardens inside its walls. Peacocks and other birds strut around as if they own the place. Also inside is **Olisipónia**, an exhibition with a 30-minute multimedia history of Lisbon and the camera obscura which has a system of lenses and mirrors, providing views of the city.

THE CATHEDRAL

Many cities tend to be built around their grand cathedral squares, but Lisbon's cathedral, **Sé Patriarcal 🐧**, (Lisbon Cathedral; daily 9am–7pm, Sun until 8pm), appears out of nowhere at a bend in the road. It is most easily reached from the centre by continuing east on the extension of Rua da Conceição. Despite the lack of pomp and circumstance, this handsome building has significant historic and artistic importance. Begun as a fortress-church in the 12th century, its towers and walls suggest a citadel. The church suffered earthquake damage during the 14th, 16th and 18th centuries, but it retains its Romanesque facade. The 13th-century cloister gardens have been excavated to reveal signs of Iron Age, Roman and Moorish occupation all on this same site. A **Roman amphitheatre** has been uncovered just above the site.

A few steps down the hill from the cathedral, the little **Igreja de Santo António da Sé** (www.stoantoniolisboa.com), built in 1812, honours Lisbon's revered native son, known throughout the world as St Anthony of Padua. The crypt – all that survived the 1755 earthquake – was built on the spot where, according to local lore, St Anthony's house stood. He is the patron saint of women looking for husbands; sometimes, bridal bouquets are left at his altar in the cathedral, along with thanks for all of his good work. It's worth looking in the **Santo António Museum** (www.museude lisboa.pt; Tue–Sun 10am– 6pm) next to the church.

Towards the waterfront, at Campo das Cebolas, the **Casa dos Bicos,** faced with sharp pyramid-shaped stones, dates from the early 16th century. It Belonged to the illegitimate son of Afonso de Albuquerque, the viceroy of Portuguese India. It is now the seat of the **José Saramago Foundation** (www.jose saramago.org), a private institution dedicated to

Casa dos Bicos

Museu Nacional do Azulejo

the life and work of José Saramago, Portugal's first Literature Nobel Prize winner. It's also a branch of the Museu de Lisboa (www.museudelisboa.pt Tue–Sat 10am–6pm).

The **Rua dos Bacalhoeiros** (Street of Cod-Sellers), on which the house stands, has various small *tascas* (restaurants) and the Loja dos Descobrimentos handicraft shop (www.loja-descobrimentos.com), specialising in hand-painted tiles. The west end of the street leads to the busy waterfront square, Praça do Comércio.

A DETOUR EAST: TWO MUSEUMS

Along the riverfront just to the east of Alfama are two important museums. The **Museu Militar** (Military Museum; Tue–Sun 10am–5pm), in a large building across the square from the Santa Apolónia railway station, is on the site of a foundry where cannon were cast during the 16th century. Among the exhibits is Vasco da Gama's two-handed sword, almost as tall as a man, relics of the Napoleonic Wars and mementoes of Portugal's last skirmishes in its colonies.

A short way beyond is the marvellous, light-filled **Museu Nacional do Azulejo** ❼ (National Tile Museum; www.museu doazulejo.pt; Tue-Sun 10am–6pm), devoted entirely to the art of the painted ceramic tiles that are on view everywhere in Portugal. The museum occupies much of the former Manueline Convento da Madre de Deus (1509), and includes a small double-decker cloister surrounded by tiles in Moorish-style geometric patterns. It is filled with around 12,000 beautiful *azulejos*, ranging from 15th-century polychrome designs to contemporary examples.

One treasure is the *Lisbon Panorama*, a 36m- (118ft-) long composition of blue-and-white painted tiles, recording Lisbon's riverside as it looked 25 years before the 1755 earthquake. Another is the fabulous interior of the small church of Igreja da Madre de Deus, an interesting mix of rococo gilt and gorgeous *azulejos*. Side walls are adorned with blue-and-white tiles from The Netherlands; two rows of enormous paintings hang above them, and the ceiling also serves as a giant canvas.

BAIXA (LOWER CITY)

Praça do Comércio ⓼ (Commerce Square) is a rare extravagant touch in understated Lisbon. Stately arcades and bold yellow government buildings line three sides of the vast square; the fourth is open to the river, with Venetian-style marble steps leading down to the water. On the east side of the steps is the Terreiro do Paço terminal for ferries to the opposite shore (see page 122). Ferries also leave from Cais do Sodré to the west.

Terreiro do Paço (Palace Square) was the name of this square during the four centuries when the Royal Ribeira Palace stood here, and many *Lisboetas* still use this name today, but the 1755 earthquake wiped out the entire complex of palatial buildings. The post-quake layout is harmonious and stately, but it remains part of many citizens' daily lives. They catch buses and trams here, while children play around temporary exhibitions and installations.

The Praça do Comércio has been the backdrop for some of history's dramas: King Carlos I and his son were killed here by an assassin in 1908, and this is where the first uprising of the Carnation Revolution of 1974 was staged.

On the west side, at Rua do Arsenal 15, is the **Lisboa Welcome Centre** (www.visitlisboa.com) , the city's main tourist office and the new **Lisboa Story Centre** (www.lisboastorycentre.pt; daily 10am–8pm); a fun audio-visual exhibition of the city's history. In the middle of the square is the bronze equestrian statue of José I, patron of the Marquês de Pombal, who designed the square as the centrepiece of his post-earthquake reconstruction. Another sculptural flourish is the triumphal arch, depicting the Marquês de Pombal and the explorer Vasco da Gama, and connecting government buildings on the north of the square.

The arch leads to the pedestrianised **Rua Augusta**, the main thoroughfare of Pombal's 18th-century grid and an attractive shopping street. Tiled façades and Art Nouveau touches are a feature of these 15 earthquake-proof side streets, which are full of intriguing shops, banks and small restaurants. The parallel Rua de Prata and Rua do Ouro (Silver and Gold Streets) are named after the original specialist shops in the area.

At No. 24 lies the exceptional **MUDE-Museu do Design e da Moda** ❾ (Design and Fashion Museum; www.mude.pt; closed for restauration), Europe's

Foodies' paradise

The city's main market, Mercado da Ribeira, is a colourful place selling an amazing array of fresh produce, including fish landed at the nearby Ribeira dock. In 2014 the Time Out Market opened here (Sun–Wed 10am–midnight, Thu–Sat till 2am). It has become a foodies' paradise with some of the best chefs in Portugal acquiring stalls.

leading museum of 20th-century design. It contains an incredible collection of furniture, industrial design and couture, including items by Charles Eames, Frank Gehry, Phillipe Starck, Balenciaga and Yves Saint Laurent.

On the west side of the Baixa is the Bairro Alto, the 'Upper Quarter', which is easily scaled by the **Elevador de Santa Justa** (www.carris.pt; daily 7am–9pm, in summer until 11pm; viewpoint from 9am), a 30m- (100ft-) high iron neo-Gothic lift built by Raúl Mesnier in 1902. Originally powered by steam, it was rebuilt in 1993. An upper gangway gives access to the Bairro Alto. Today the still-functioning lift takes people to the level just below the top, from where a spiral staircase leads up to the main observation deck, with its pleasant café and sensational views of Lisbon's tiled rooftops and the São Jorge castle.

Take the Elevador de Santa Justa for stunning views of Lisbon

The steps behind the lift lead up to emerge at the gently sloping **Rua do Carmo**, with a blend of modern and traditional shops. The latter include the **Luvaria Ulisses** (www.luvaria ulisses.com), a glove shop with an Art-Deco street frontage that is barely a metre wide.

ROSSIO

Turn left up Rua do Carmo to enter the Chiado district (see page 45), or follow it down to the right to emerge on the **Rossio** ⓫

Estação do Rossio

(formally named Praça Dom Pedro IV), Lisbon's main square, once the scene of public hangings, bullfights and the burning of the Inquisition's victims. Today, the square is still one of the main centres of activity in Lisbon – it's a great place to window-shop, meet friends, watch the busy crowds go by from pavement cafés, such as the Art Nouveau **Nicola**, and listen to the fountains.

The statue on the column in the square honours the first emperor of Brazil, Pedro IV (1826–34). On the northern end of the square is the handsome **Teatro Nacional Dona Maria II** (www. tndm.pt). Just beyond the theatre on the right are a couple of *ginjinha* (cherry brandy) kiosks, which make the area an evening gathering place. Nearby is the southern end of **Rua das Portas de Santo Antão**, a street bustling with lively restaurant tables, much appreciated by patrons of the popular **Teatro Politeama** up on the left. At No. 58 is the **Casa do Alentejo**. Once the property of the counts of Alverca, it is unassuming from the outside, but as you go through the entrance and up the steps you're confronted by a riot of interior styling: an attractive Moorish courtyard with Art Deco flourishes, and on the first floor, a traditional restaurant with massed panels of vivid *azulejos*, serving excellent Alentejo dishes at reasonable prices (www.casadoalentejo.com.pt).

On the west side of the square, one street removed, is the **Estação do Rossio**, the railway station from where local trains run to Sintra and Mafra (see pages 66 and 71). Its horse-shoe arches make it look like a Moorish palace, but it is a romantic effort of the late 19th century.

To the east of Rossio is another major square, **Praça da Figueira**, which is another hub for buses and the No. 12 tram. At its centre is a statue of João I, founder of the Avis dynasty. Just to the northeast is **Praça Martim Moniz**, decked with fountains that function as a water park for children. The views of Alfama and the castle district from here are lovely.

The road past Rossio station opens out into **Praça dos Restauradores** (Square of the Restoration), where an obelisk celebrates the overthrow of Spanish rule in 1640. **Palácio Foz**, the once splendid pink palace on the west side of the square beside the former Art Deco Teatro Eden, now houses a **tourist information office** Ask me Lisboa (www.visit lisboa.com). Just beyond it,

Praça dos Restauradores

A quiet moment in Jardim Botânico

the Elevador da Glória funicular takes you up to the Bairro Alto (see page 42).

From this point, **Avenida da Liberdade** makes its way uphill for a little over 1km (0.5 mile). The stately boulevard of upmarket shops is graced with statues, fountains, ponds, flower gardens, promenade cafés and benches. The boulevard ends at the **Praça Marquês de Pombal** (or Rotunda) traffic hub from which an elevated statue of Pombal, accompanied by a lion, looks out over his rebuilt Lisbon.

BAIRRO ALTO (UPPER CITY)

Like the steep Alfama district, the Bairro Alto is a hilly and dense area full of picturesque old houses, their wrought-iron balconies hung with birdcages and flowerpots. Half asleep during the day, Bairro Alto is the nightlife epicentre of Lisbon. After dark, the sad songs of *fado* nightclubs spill out into the cobbled streets.

The easiest way to reach the Bairro Alto is to board the **Elevador da Glória**, the yellow funicular trolley at Praça dos Restauradores. Locals, however, are as apt to walk up the hill as wait for the funicular. At the top end of the brief journey is a lookout park, **Miradouro de São Pedro de Alcântara**, with an excellent view of the Castelo de São Jorge across the Baixa.

Opposite the top of the funicular, on the ground floor of the 18th-century Palace of São Pedro de Alcântara, is the **Solar do Vinho do Porto ⑫** (Port and Douro Wines Institute; www. ivdp.pt; Mon–Fri 11am–midnight, Sat 3pm-midnight), where you can sample the famous Portuguese wines.

North of the *miradouro*, along Rua de São Pedro de Alcântara, lies the **Jardim Botânico** (Botanical Garden; summer daily 9am–8pm, winter Mon–Fri 9am–5pm, Sat–Sun until 6pm), reached through the university gate alongside the Academy of Sciences; it is part of the Museu National de História Natural e da Ciencia (www.museus.ulisboa.pt). It concentrates on the scientific cultivation of unusual plants from distant climes, but this serious activity doesn't disturb the lush, slightly unkempt beauty and tranquillity. The tree-shaded gardens slope steeply downhill to a lower gate near the Avenida Metro station.

SÃO ROQUE AND CARMO CHURCHES

Two churches in the upper town are unusual enough to merit a visit. Just down Rua de São Pedro do Alcântara, turning left from the top of the funicular, is Largo Trindade Coelho and the **Igreja de São Roque ⑬**. The church's dull exterior (the original 16th-century façade perished in the 1755 earthquake) conceals the most lavishly decorated chapel in Lisbon: the baroque altar of the chapel of São João Baptista (St John the Baptist) is a wealth of gold, silver, bronze, agate, amethyst, lapis lazuli, ivory and Carrara marble. In 1742, João V of Portugal sent orders for this altar to Rome, where teams of artists and artisans worked on it for five years. After the Pope had given his blessing, the prefabricated masterpiece was dismantled and shipped to the customer. The church ceiling, from 1589, is the only surviving example in Lisbon of a Mannerist painted ceiling. Adjoining the church, the impressive **Museu de Arte Sacra** (Museum of Sacred Art; www.museusaoroque.com; Apr–Sep Mon 2–7pm, Tue–Sun 10am–7pm, Fri until 8pm, Oct–Mar daily until 6pm) contains a collection of beautifully presented precious reliquaries, paintings, delicately worked jewellery and vestments.

The Bairro Alto's restaurants and bars are in the side streets to the west of Rua de São Pedro de Alcântara. For a daylight impression of the narrow streets with their overhanging balconies, take a walk from Largo Trindade Coelho up the **Travessa da Queimada**. The streets are in a grid pattern, so it's easy to explore and navigate your way back.

From Largo Trindade Coelho, you can also walk downhill towards the Chiado district, via **Rua Nova da Trindade**. Halfway down on the left is the **Cervejeria da Trindade**, an old beer hall decorated with *azulejos*, where you can enjoy hearty food (the seafood is excellent) at reasonable prices (see page 107).

If you continue to the bottom and turn left, you'll arrive at Largo do Carmo, where the **Igreja do Carmo** ⑭ (Carmelite Church) is rich only in memories. Today it stands in ruins, a mere shell, but is an evocative reminder of the 1755 earthquake's tremendous destruction – the roof fell in on a full congregation on All Saints' Day. The foundations date to the 14th century. Housed inside the only part of the church that has a roof over it is the **Museu Archeológico do Carmo** (www.museuarqueologicodocarmo.pt; Mon–Sat 10am–6pm, June–Sept until

7pm). This small archaeological museum has a collection that includes prehistoric pottery, some Roman sculptures, early Portuguese tombs and even a few ancient mummies under glass.

Window shopping in Chiado

CHIADO AND SÃO BENTO PALACE

The streets of chic **Chiado** have long been renowned for dispensing Lisbon's most elegant goods – silverware, leather, fashions and books – along with fine pastry and tea shops. The main commercial street, with some high-end fashion shops, is **Rua Garrett**, where a statue of the poet Fernando Pessoa sits outside **Café A Brasileira**, which has attracted artists for a century.

In 1988 part of Chiado was devastated by fires that wiped out two of Europe's oldest department stores, including the legendary Armazéns do Chiado (www.armazensdochiado.com). Portugal's most famous architect, the modernist Álvaro Siza, oversaw the tastefully preserved reconstruction of the neighbourhood, especially along Rua do Carmo (see page 39). On the **Largo Barão Quintela**, just off Rua do Alecrim, is another statue, this one of the 19th-century novelist Eça de Queiroz, gazing upon a naked muse.

The **Museu do Chiado** (www.museuartecontemporanea. gov.pt; Tue–Sun 10am–6pm), in the former San Francisco Convent on Rua Serpa Pinto, houses an impressive collection of

Portuguese art from the late 19th century to the present.

West of the Bairro Alto lies the **Palácio São Bento**, a former Benedictine monastery that is now home to Portugal's parliament (www.en.parlamento.pt). Beyond it is the delightful park Jardim Guerra Jumqueiro, better known as **Jardim da Estrela** after the distinguished 18th-century church across the street. This richly decorated basilica was completed in 1789. The 19th-century park contains abundant tropical foliage, plus the customary ducks, geese, peacocks and pheasants. Just beyond the park is the **Cemitério dos Ingleses** (English Cemetery), where Henry Fielding (1707–54), author of *Tom Jones*, is buried.

LAPA

Moving west and down towards the river from Chiado is the elegant residential neighbourhood of Lapa. It is home to embassies, townhouses and several intimate hotels, but to most visitors it is known as the address of the **Museu Nacional de Arte Antiga** ⓯ (National Museum of Ancient Art; www.museudearteantiga.pt; Tue–Sun 10am–6pm), Portugal's largest museum. It is housed on the site of a Carmelite convent in a large and handsomely designed palace on Rua das Janelas Verdes. On three floors, the museum is an absorbing place with at least several masterpieces of international renown.

On the ground floor (Piso 1) a whole glittering salon is dedicated to textiles and furniture, plus paintings by foreign artists, including Tiepolo, Fragonard and, most strikingly, the Spaniard Francisco de Zurbarán, whose six larger-than-life saints once belonged to the monastery of São Vicente de Fora (see page 32).

The same floor also has a triptych – both entertaining and horrific – by Hieronymus Bosch (1450–1516), the Flemish artist who painted surreal allegorical scenes with alien-like creatures. *The Temptation of St Anthony*, painted around 1500, is a fantastic hallucination, tempered with humour and executed with mad genius. A crane rigged up like a helicopter, flying fish taxis and horse-size rats fill this ghoulish nightmare.

The second floor contains oriental art, much of it dating from the discoveries of the 15th and 16th centuries. Two Japanese lacquer screens depict the moment that the Portuguese – the first Europeans – landed in Japan. The new arrivals are depicted as villains up to no good, while the locals watch, amused, from their balconies.

The top floor is devoted to Portuguese art and sculpture. Here a highlight is *The Adoration of St Vincent*, a multi-panel work also taken from São Vicente de Fora monastery and attributed to the 15th-century Portuguese master, Nuno Gonçalves. It is a spectacular portrait of contemporary dignitaries, including Henry the Navigator. Dozens of others are shown in every range of

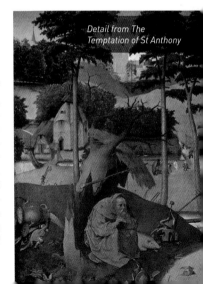

Detail from The Temptation of St Anthony

Custard tarts

The Belém district is famous for its special pastries (*pastéis de Belém*) – custard tarts coated with icing sugar and cinnamon. The best, made to a secret recipe, are those sold at the Pastéis de Belém (see page 110), at Rua de Belém, No. 84–92.

distracção – ire, boredom and amusement – while several of the assembled clergymen appear as ugly, evil or both.

There is a pleasant garden and café, and the museum looks out over the **Doca do Alcântara**, where the **Fragata *D. Fernando II e Glória*** is berthed (http://ccm.marinha.pt/pt/d fernando; Tue–Sun 10am–5pm, May–Sept until 6pm, Mon opens at noon). This beautiful vessel, the Portuguese navy's last sailing ship, was built in the Indian colony of Damão in 1843. The dock's brightly painted **Estação Maritima de Alcântara**, with murals by José Almada Negreiros, is where cruise-ship passengers come ashore. There are a number of bars and clubs in the terminal and around the dock, where there are also a couple of floating restaurants. The **Museu do Oriente** (www.museudooriente.pt; Tue–Sun 10am–6pm, Fri until 10pm, free Fri 6–10pm), housed in a former fish warehouse, has an interesting collection examining Portugal's historical links with Asia.

The quay of the smaller **Doca de Santo Amaro** yachting marina, just beneath Ponte 25 de April, is lined with restaurants.

BELÉM

Belém (Portuguese for Bethlehem), Lisbon's primary monumental district, is a suburb about 6km (4 miles) west of Praça do Comércio, where land reclaimed from the river has been

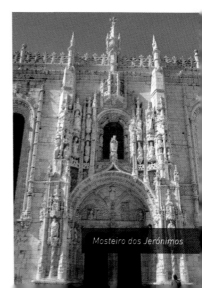

fashioned into parkland, new cultural centres and marinas. Though the shore has changed beyond recognition, it was from here that the great Portuguese voyages of discovery set out in the 15th and 16th centuries.

Tram 15 makes the waterfront trip to Belém from Praça do Comércio; bus No. 201 from Cais do Sodré (just west of Praça do Comércio) covers virtually the same route but ends up at Linda-a-Velha.

Start a visit to Belém at the edge closest to central Lisbon.

MAAT

The newest addition to the riverside is the ultramodern wave-like organic building of the **Museum of Art, Architecture and Technology ⑯** (MAAT; www.maat.pt; Wed–Mon 11am–7pm) designed by the British architect Amanda Levete. It exhibits the work of contemporary artists, architects and the treasures of the EDP Foundation's Art Collection. The museum also includes the complex of the Tejo Power Station with fine examples of the last century industrial architecture and the interesting Electricity Museum.

The interesting **Museu Nacional dos Coches** (National Coach Museum; http://museudoscoches.gov.pt; Tue–Sun 10am–6pm)

Mosteiro dos Jerónimos

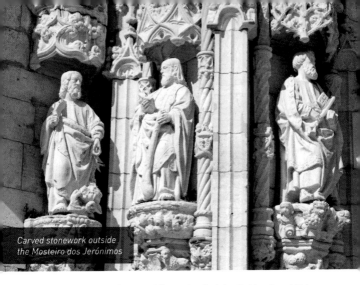

Carved stonework outside
the Mosteiro dos Jerónimos

is housed in the former riding school of the Belém Royal Palace and a new building designed by the Pritzker Prize winner, Brazilian architect Paulo Mendes da Rocha (2015). It displays dozens of impressive carriages, drawn by royal horses for ceremonial occasions over four centuries, both in the city and across the country. The most extravagant are three sculpted, gilt carriages used by the Portuguese Embassy in Rome in the early 18th century.

MOSTEIRO DOS JERÓNIMOS

A short distance away, on the Calçada da Ajuda, sits the rose-coloured official residence of the president of the Republic, **Palácio da Ajuda ⑰** (www.palacioajuda.gov.pt; Thu–Tue 10am–6pm), the biggest palace inside the city limits. Work began on the former royal residence in 1802 to replace the temporary wooden palace erected here after the earthquake. Soon after, in 1807, the royal family fled to Brazil. Work ceased until the reign of Luís I (1861–89) and his Italian bride, Princess Maria Pia of Savoy. They finished building the palace and furnished it with lavish trappings including Gobelins tapestries, oriental ceramics, crystal chandeliers and rare Portuguese furniture.

Only a short stroll westwards along the Rua de Belém is Lisbon's largest and most impressive religious monument, the **Mosteiro dos Jerónimos** ⓲ (Monastery of the Hieronymites; www.mosteirojeronimos.gov.pt; Tue–Sun 10am–5.30pm, May–Sept until 6.30pm), a Unesco World Heritage Site. Commissioned by Manuel I with the windfall of riches brought

⊙ MANUELINE ARCHITECTURE

The Portuguese may be principally known for *azulejo* designs and port wine, but equally important is the ornate style of architecture and stone carving that suddenly appeared in Portugal in the late 15th century. It flourished for only a few decades, mostly during the reign of Manuel I (1495–1521), for which it was christened Manueline.

Probably triggered by the great ocean voyages of discovery, it took late Gothic as a base and added fanciful decoration, dramatic touches that were frequently references to the sea. Stone was carved like knotted rope and sculpted into imitation coral, seahorses, nets and waves, as well as non-nautical designs. The style first appeared in the small Igreja de Jesus in Setúbal, Lisbon's Torre de Belém and the Mosteiro dos Jerónimos. The style reached a peak of complexity in the unfinished chapels of the monastery at Batalha, between Lisbon and Coimbra. In the early 16th century, the style fell out of favour, and by 1540 Portugal had joined the rest of Europe in building in the more sober Renaissance style.

back by Portuguese ships from the East, the monastery is an obvious testament to a confident and faithful nation. The convent wing was destroyed in the 1755 earthquake, but the church and cloister survived, classic examples of 16th-century style.

The vast south façade of the church, parallel to the river, is mostly unadorned limestone, making the few embellishments all the more remarkable. The main portal is a brilliant example of intricately carved stonework, as are the church's tall Manueline columns (this style bridged the gap between the Gothic and Renaissance styles in Portugal). The effect is one of immense height and space. The first architect in charge was a Frenchman, Diogo Boitac, who was succeeded by the Spaniard Juan de Castillo, responsible for the cloister and main portal.

Inside the church are the royal tombs of Manuel I, his wife Dona Maria, and others, set on pompous sculptured elephants, a tribute to the newly discovered marvels of the East. Near the west door are the modern tombs of two giants of Portugal's Golden Age, Vasco da Gama and the poet Luís de Camões.

Once you leave the church (don't miss the fine sculptural work surrounding the exterior of the main door), turn right and visit the **cloister**, an airy two-level structure of strikingly original proportions and perspectives. Note the clever intersection of both sharp angles and arches. No two columns are the same.

Centro Cultural

Across the road from the Jerónimos Monastery is the Centro Cultural de Belém, built in 1992. It houses the fantastic Museu Colecção Berardo, with a superb collection of modern art, stages temporary exhibitions, and holds concerts in its auditoriums. With shops and cafés, it is well worth visiting to find out what events are taking place.

MONASTERY MUSEUMS

The south section of the monastery has been restored and forms a beautiful setting for the **Museu Nacional de Arqueologia** ⑲ (National Museum of Archaeology; www.museu arqueologia.gov.pt; Tue–Sun 10am–6pm), an important collection of ancient relics, including Stone Age tools, Bronze Age jewels, Roman sculptures and mosaics, and some exqui-

Padrão dos Descobrimentos

site medieval carving, most breathtaking of which is a tomb depicting Jesus and St Francis.

Portugal's fascinating maritime heritage is documented at the **Museu da Marinha** (Maritime Museum; daily 10am–5pm, May–Sept until 6pm), which is housed in the west and northern wings of the monastery and in new buildings around the square opposite the entrance. Among the museum's collection are hundreds of models of various ship types through the ages, and numerous artefacts such as naval uniforms, maps and navigation equipment.

Also on display is a delightful sculpture of the archangel Raphael that accompanied Vasco da Gama on his first voyage of exploration in 1497. Of more recent date are the handsome royal suites from the *Amália*, the 1901 royal yacht that belonged to King Carlos I, who was an amateur marine biologist. Pride of place goes to the huge galliot, or brigantine, built in 1785 to celebrate

Torre de Belém

a royal marriage, with seats for 80 oarsmen. The last time it was on the River Tagus was in 1957, carrying Queen Elizabeth II of Britain on a state visit. Next to it is the seaplane piloted by Portuguese aviators that in 1922 made the first flight across the South Atlantic. The educational attractions continue with a **Planetário Calouste Gulbenkian**. Both the museum and the planetarium form part of the **Centro de Conhecimento do Mar** (Maritime Knowledge Center; http://ccm.marinha.pt).

BERARDO'S MUSEUM AND THE DISCOVERIES MONUMENT

In the arts hub that is the **Centro Cultural de Belém** (www. ccb.pt), the **Museu Colecção Berardo 20** (Berardo Collection Museum; Praça do Império; www.museuberardo.pt; daily 10am–7pm; free on Sat) displays the incredible modern art collection of billionaire José Berardo against gleaming white walls, with a roll call of contemporary greats, including Andy Warhol, Paula Rego, Roy Lichenstein and more.

The arresting **Padrão dos Descobrimentos 21** (Monument to the Discoveries; www.padraodosdescobrimentos.pt; daily Mar–Sept 10am–7pm, Tue–Sun Oct–Feb 10am–6pm), built in 1960 to commemorate the 500th anniversary of Henry the Navigator's death, juts from the riverbank like a caravel cresting a wave.

On the prow stands Prince Henry, looking out across the river and wearing, as always, his distinctive round hat. The figures behind him represent noted explorers, crusaders, astronomers, cartographers, chroniclers and others instrumental in Portugal's Age of Discovery. A lift followed by stairs leads to the top and a superb view.

TORRE DE BELÉM

Finally, there is the Unesco World Heritage Site, **Torre de Belém** ㉒ (Tower of Belém; www.torrebelem.pt; Tue–Sun Oct–Apr 10am–5.30pm, May–Sept until 6.30pm), erected in 1515 to defend the entry to Lisbon. This fortress is one of the finest examples of Manueline architecture, with its battlements, corner turrets and stonework featuring the repeated theme of the Cross. After crossing the wooden bridge, climb several floors to a top-level terrace that looks out over the Tagus.

NORTH LISBON

At the north end of Avenida da Liberdade, beyond the Marquês de Pombal rotunda, is a formal park, **Parque Eduardo VII**, its well-manicured lawns and shrubs flanked by wooded areas and gardens. So thrilled were the Portuguese by a royal visit at the turn of the 20th century that they named the park after Britain's king, Edward VII.

Lisbon's most original botanical triumph occupies the northwest corner of the park. Known as **Estufa Fria** ㉓ (the Cold House; http://estufafria.cm-lisboa.pt; daily Oct–Mar 9am–5pm, Apr–Sept 10am–7pm), this garden was created in the early 20th century on the site of a quarry, and it owes its name to the fact that its simple wooden lath roof gives shade but no heat, allowing plants from a variety of backgrounds to grow as naturally as possible, protected from the Lisboan extremes of climate. Paths weave their way through the enormous space among species from Africa, Asia and South America. At the far side, a doorway leads through to the cavernous **Estufa Quente** (the Hot House), which was built at the end of the 1950s on the highest point of the quarry. Its roof and walls are made of glass, to capture the maximum

⊙ CALOUSTE GULBENKIAN

At the dawn of the Oil Age, a far-sighted Turkish-born Armenian put up money to help finance drilling in Mesopotamia (now Iraq), then part of the Turkish Empire. For his part, he received 5 percent of the Iraq Petroleum Company. Two world wars and the fuelling of millions of cars, planes and ships made Calouste Gulbenkian rich beyond imagination. He became a knowledgeable and dedicated collector of antiquities and great art, beginning with Turkish and Persian carpets, Armenian and Arabic manuscripts, and Greek and Roman coins. His passions spread to include ancient Egyptian art, Chinese porcelain and Western painting. His mission was acquiring perfect examples in each of his chosen fields.

Gulbenkian (who had British nationality for much of his life) was preparing to travel to the United States when he fell ill in Lisbon. He was so impressed with his treatment here that he decided to stay, establishing a philanthropic foundation to which he left most of his money and his collections when he died in 1955. The Gulbenkian Museum is his centrepiece, complemented by several other cultural facilities in Portugal, including the Modern Art Centre, regional museums, a planetarium and educational institutes.

amount of light and heat, so that more tropical species can thrive here.

MUSEU GULBENKIAN

To the north of Parque Eduardo VII, off Avenida António Augusto Aguiar, is one of the world's great museums, **Museu Gulbenkian** (Gulbenkian Museum; Avenida da Berna 45; https://gulbenkian.pt; Wed–Mon 10am–6pm). It was created to house one of the finest private art collections in Europe, acquired by an Armenian billionaire, Calouste Gulbenkian, and later bequeathed to the Portuguese state. A great philanthropist who died in Lisbon in 1955, Gulbenkian meticulously acquired acclaimed masterpieces and built up an excellent and wide-ranging collection.

Exhibit at Museu Gulbenkian

Surrounded by its own perfectly planned and maintained 17-acre park, the museum houses a huge collection, which begins chronologically, with Egyptian ceramics and sculptures dating back to around 2700BC, delicate and perfectly preserved. The handsome statue of the judge Bes is inscribed with hieroglyphs that date it from the reign of Pharaoh Psamtik I (7th century BC).

A large section of the museum is devoted to art of the Islamic East, and includes ancient fabrics, costumes and carpets, ceramics, glassware and illuminated pages from the Koran. The survey of Western art begins in the 11th century

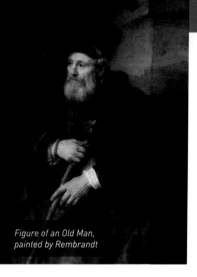

Figure of an Old Man, painted by Rembrandt

with illuminated parchment manuscripts. Tiny ivory sculptures of religious scenes come from 14th-century France, and there are a number of well-preserved tapestries from the Flemish and Italian workshops of the 16th century.

Paintings by Dutch and Flemish masters include works by Hals, Van Dyck and Ruysdael. Pride of place is given to two Rembrandts: *Figure of an Old Man* and a painting of a helmeted warrior believed to be Pallas Athene or Alexander the Great, probably modelled by Rembrandt's son Titus.

The impressive hall of Chinese porcelain begins with the Yuan dynasty (13th–14th century; around the time of Marco Polo) and goes on to some exquisite items from the 17th and 18th centuries. Miraculously unmarred by the forces of time, each object is representative of the pinnacle of a particular school of art.

The last room of the museum contains 169 items by Gulbenkian's friend René Lalique (1860–1945), the talented and versatile French jeweller. On display are exquisite Art Nouveau combs, pendants, bracelets and necklaces, including a dazzling, bejewelled brooch of nine entwined serpents.

The **Centro de Arte Moderna** ㉕ (Modern Art Centre; as above; a combined ticket with the main museum is available) is also a part of the Gulbenkian Foundation. This is the best place to see 20th-century Portuguese and British art, and there are some excellent works by Amadeo de Souza Cardoso, Vieira da Silva and Almada Negreiros, particularly of society types and Lisbon café life. There are a couple of early Paula Rego abstracts, from 1935, and works by British artists such as David Hockney and Henry Moore.

The Foundation has exhibition spaces and concert halls where musical performances and ballets take place. There is also a library, with occasional free Sunday lunchtime concerts, a bookshop and a restaurant.

AQUEDUTO DAS ÁGUAS LIVRES

A landmark that is most often seen by those heading out of town is the soaring arches of **Aqueduto das Águas Livres** ㉖ (a freshwater aqueduct), which spans an impressive 18km (11 miles) across the Alcântara valley north of downtown Lisbon. Fresh water was first carried across the aqueduct in 1748 and, since it managed to survive the earthquake, it continues to flow. A visit to the aqueduct can be arranged through the **Museu de Água** (Water Museum; www.epal.pt; Tue–Sat 10am–5.30pm) in the city's first steam-pumping station, in Rua do Alviela near Santa Apolónia station.

Along with the motorway to Cascais, the aqueduct slices through the city's biggest park, **Monsanto**. Eucalyptus, cypress, cedar, umbrella pines and oak trees all thrive on the rolling hillsides. Apart from calm and fresh air, the park contains leisure and sports grounds, bars and restaurants. Its municipal camping ground ranks as one of Europe's prettiest and best organised, and the park also has some impressive *miradouros*, giving outstanding views over Lisbon and the estuary.

Futuristic architecture at Parque das Nações

PARQUE DAS NAÇÕES

Lisbon, and the whole of Portugal, pinned much hope on the city's hosting of the World Expo in 1998. Celebrating the 'Heritage of the Oceans', it was an opportunity for the nation to pay tribute to its former maritime greatness and reintroduce itself to the world.

Lisbon used the occasion to reinvigorate a run-down industrial area east of the city, creating a high-tech entertainment park, along with new shopping and nightlife areas. Framing the park is the futuristic railway station, **Estação do Oriente**, designed by the Spanish architect Santiago Calatrava as a major terminal for destinations around the country, a pristine shopping mall and the stark white Ponte Vasco da Gama (Vasco da Gama Bridge) extending across the Tagus into the horizon – Europe's longest bridge at 17.2km (10.75 miles).

The **Parque das Nações** (Nations' Park; www.portaldasna coes.pt) complex extends 5km (3 miles) along the riverfront, principally drawing visitors to its world-class aquarium, which served as the Oceans Pavilion during the Expo, and has since become one of the city's primary attractions.

The complex won the award for best urban development in Iberia in 1999. Designed by the American Peter Chermayeff, the **Oceanário de Lisboa** ㉗ (www.oceanario.pt; daily 10am– 7pm, summer until 8pm), resembling a marooned oil der- rick or space station from the set of a sci-fi thriller, is one of the largest and finest aquariums in the world. Reached by a footbridge, it houses large tanks representing four distinct marine ecosystems – Antarctic, Indian, Pacific and Atlantic – with more than 10,000 examples of marine life in 200 spe- cies, taken from across the world. You'll see penguins in the Antarctic section and otters in the Pacific. As visitors make their way around the massive circular aquarium, the size of four Olympic-size swimming pools, tiger sharks, manta rays and schools of brightly coloured fish glide silently by, overhead and beneath the observation decks.

Nations' Park is a good place for families. There are whimsi- cal fountains, paddle boats, garden playgrounds, bowling lanes, aerial cable cars running the length of the waterfront, and the **Torre Vasco da Gama**, a tower with an observation deck – the tallest structure in Portugal – that looks out to the Atlantic and back down the river at Lisbon.

The **Pavilhão do Conhe- cimento** (the Pavilion of

Park panorama

A high point of the Parque das Nações is the 145m (475ft) Torre Vasco da Gama, with a panoramic view from the terrace and restaurant in the 'crow's nest' 104m (341ft) above ground.

Cycling by Ponte 25 de Abril

Knowledge; www.pavconhecimento.pt; Tue–Fri 10am–6pm, Sat–Sun 11am–7pm), is a thrilling, highly-educational, hands-on museum of science and technology.

Sporting events, such as basketball and tennis, and concerts by big-name international and local performers, are held at the mushroom-like **Atlântico Hall** arena (Altice Arena), which functioned as the Utopia Pavilion during the Expo. The **Teatro Camões** is home to the excellent national ballet company (www.cnb.pt).

Many restaurants and bars have moved into the marina area, transforming it into an animated nightspot, and the construction of hotels and residential housing are creating a desirable suburb. The mall around the Metro station attracts late-night and Sunday shoppers.

Among the former pavilions notable for their architectural interest is the **Portugal Pavilion** beside the marina, by the

Pritzker prize-winning Portuguese architect Álvaro Siza Vieira. The pavilion has an astonishing curved and suspended roof 67m (221ft) long and weighing 1,400 tonnes.

ACROSS THE TAGUS

With a span of 2.3km (1.5 miles), the **Ponte 25 de Abril** ❷❽ across the River Tagus became the longest suspension bridge in Europe when it was opened in 1966. Originally named in honour of the nation's dictator, after the revolution of 1974 the name 'Salazar' was removed, and for quite a time it was known simply as 'the bridge'. In an about-face, it was renamed after the date of the Carnation Revolution. Though its bold red colour is quite striking, the bridge lacks the grace of the Golden Gate Bridge in San Francisco, with which it is often compared.

Just across the river, above Cacilhas and looming up over the bridge's tollbooths, is Lisbon's take on Rio de Janeiro's landmark, the enormous **statue of Cristo Rei** (Christ the King), built in 1959. Almost 30m (100ft) tall, it stands on a pedestal that is another 82m (269ft) high.

A chapel, the Santuário de Cristo Rei (http://cristorei.pt), is housed in the base of the towering monument, where there is also a cafeteria. Take the lift up to the viewing terrace at the top of the pedestal for a glorious 360-degree panoramic view of the estuary, the bridge, all of Lisbon and a vast expanse of Portugal to the south, including the Serra da Arrábida (see page 79).

Reaching Cristo Rei

To visit the statue of Cristo Rei you can drive across the bridge or take one of the orange ferries from Cais do Sodré to Cacilhas and then a taxi or a bus marked 'Cristo Rei'.

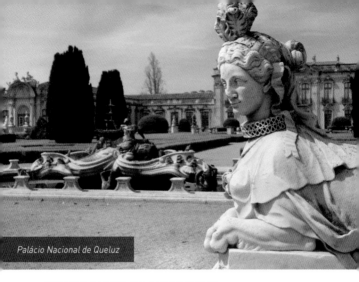

Palácio Nacional de Queluz

EXCURSIONS FROM LISBON

One of the great attractions of Lisbon is the fact that a number of desirable excursions are only a very short distance from the capital – there are highlights west, south and north of the city. Whether you're looking for grand palaces, beach resorts, awe-inspiring abbeys or a charming romantic town lodged in the mountains, there's plenty to explore in the environs.

QUELUZ

An easy half-day outing is to **Palácio Nacional de Queluz** ㉙ (www.parquesdesintra.pt; daily 9am–6pm), 14km (9 miles) west of Lisbon. To reach it, take a bus tour or a commuter train from Rossio station to Queluz-Belas. By car it's 20 minutes on the motorway through the forest of Monsanto; the turn-off on the way to Sintra is clearly signposted. You're hardly out of Lisbon's mushrooming suburbs before you're alongside the elegant palace.

Pedro III commissioned this sumptuous, pretty pink summer palace, which was built in the second half of the 18th century by the Frenchman Jean-Baptiste Robillon and the Portuguese Mateus Vicente de Oliveira. As a working official residence for the royal family, Queluz thrived mostly during the reign of Maria I (1777–99), Pedro III's wife. The queen suffered from bouts of depression, which deepened into madness, and visitors to the palace told of her shrieking fits.

From the road, the palace seems relatively unprepossessing, but inside, Portuguese modesty is totally abandoned, and Queluz is a model of only slightly tattered splendour. Though the palace lost much to French invasions (it was used by General Andoche Junot as his headquarters during the Peninsular War) and a 1934 fire, it manages to preserve an air of 18th-century royal privilege. The **throne room** is one of the most lavish, with overpowering chandeliers and walls and ceilings layered with gilt. The **Sala dos Embaixadores** (Hall of Ambassadors) has a floor like a huge chessboard in addition to a wealth of mirrors and a *trompe l'oeil* ceiling.

The **Palace Gardens** are the pride of Queluz and seem never-ending, with clipped hedges in perfect geometric array, bushes barbered into inventive shapes, imaginative fountains and armies of statues. The huge old magnolia trees and orange trees close by relieve some of the formality. Royal guests once entered the garden via the pompous but original **Escadaria dos Leões** (Lions' Staircase).

In the early 19th century dozens of live animals – not just dogs, but lions and wolves – were boarded at Queluz, which was then the site of the royal zoo.

One rather original attraction is the man-made river. Enclosed between retaining walls covered in precious *azulejos*, a real stream was diverted to pass through the huge palace grounds, and was dammed so that the level of the water could be raised whenever the royal residents wanted to go for a boat ride.

The former royal kitchen has been converted into a prestigious restaurant run by the *pousada* hotel chain (www.pousadas.pt). With giant old utensils, a fireplace big enough for a crowd to walk into, and lots of atmosphere, the place is called – understandably – *Cozinha Velha*, or 'Old Kitchen'.

SINTRA

Sintra ③⓪ is a magical, palace-dotted landscape, which feels like it has sprung from a storybook. Easily reached by train from Rossio, and nestled into the Serra de Sintra, 25km (16 miles) northwest of Lisbon, it was once a coveted summer retreat for royals; today it's a romantic getaway for people from all over the world. Clustered throughout the forested hillsides are old palaces and estates with spectacular vistas. Two peaks in the range are crowned by reminders of Sintra's illustrious past: Castelo dos Mouros, the ruins of a castle built by occupying Moors in the 8th century, and Palácio de Pena, the multicoloured fantasy palace built by a German nobleman for his Portuguese wife. The views from either of these points extends as far as the sea,

> ### By train to Sintra
>
> The easiest way to reach Sintra is by train. It's also accessible by car, but the single entry road can get jammed with cars, and parking is sometimes difficult. However, a car is useful if you want to access the fish restaurants closer to the coast.

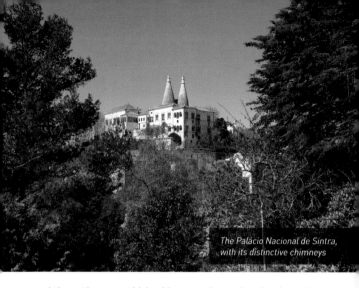

The Palácio Nacional de Sintra, with its distinctive chimneys

and the entire area, thick with vegetation and paths through the hills, provides spectacular trekking.

Right in the centre of town is the **Palácio Nacional de Sintra** (also called the *Paço Real*, or Royal Palace; www.parquesdes intra.pt; daily 9.30am–6pm). Except for its two huge, white conical chimneys, from the outside it looks like a fairly ordinary hulk of a palace. Its real treasures lie inside.

A summer home for Portuguese kings since the early 14th century, the palace's design became more and more unpredictable and haphazard as wings were added over the centuries, with back-to-back medieval and Manueline styles. The resulting interiors and furnishings are remarkable, including some of the oldest and most valuable *azulejos* in Portugal, which line many of the rooms.

Every room in the Palácio Nacional has a story to tell. During the 17th century, the dull-witted Afonso VI was pressured into

Sala dos Cisnes

abdicating for the benefit of the country, therefore allowing his more effective brother, Pedro II, to become king.

When a plot to restore Afonso to the throne was discovered, the former monarch was exiled to Sintra. For nine years, until he died in 1683, he was imprisoned in a simple room of the Palácio Nacional. It's said that the worn floor is a result of Afonso's constant pacing up and down.

A large ground-floor hall, **Sala das Pegas** (Magpie Salon), tells a very different story. João I (1385–1433) was caught by Queen Philippa kissing one of her ladies-in-waiting. The palace gossips had a field day until the king ordered the entire ceiling of the hall closed and painted with magpies, as many as there were ladies-in-waiting, 136 in fact. Each held in its beak a ribbon with the king's motto, *por bem* (in honour). The royal rebuke, the king's way of saying 'so what' and 'shut up', had the desired effect.

The so-called **Sala dos Cisnes** (Swan Room) is decorated with ceiling panels painted with swans, each in a different position. There are also ceilings with intricate designs in the *mudéjar* style influenced by Moorish art.

The palace's landmark twin chimneys, shaped like inverted cones, were used to let the smoke out of the massive kitchen when oxen were being roasted for large banquets given for visiting dignitaries.

Moors' castle and the Pena Palace

A special bus climbs a steep road with hairpin turns into the *serra* from Sintra to visit some spectacular monuments. The oldest, **Castelo dos Mouros** (Moors' Castle; www.parques-desintra.pt; daily 10am–6pm), hugs a rocky ridge overlooking the town. It was erected during the 8th century, soon after the Moors occupied Portugal. The dauntless Dom Afonso Henriques conquered it for the Christians in 1147, a major victory in the reconquest of Portugal.

Today the castle is a ruin, but a fascinating one, its crenellated walls still severe. Those with the energy to do so should climb the ramparts to the top for incredible views of the entire forested area, to the sea beyond, and across the treetops to Sintra's most famous monument, the Palácio da Pena. It's easy to pick out individual *quintas* (estates) in their privileged seclusion.

Further up the same winding road on the hilltop, the **Palácio da Pena** (www.parquesdesintra.pt; daily 10am–6pm), more than 450m (1,500ft) above sea-level, is an outrageous Victorian folly reached by way of a park so lush with flowering trees and vines

---

⊘ SINTRA'S COUNTRY MARKET

On the second and last Sunday of each month, a country fair is held in São Pedro do Sintra, a village adjacent to Sintra – be prepared to encounter traffic jams. The origins of the fair go back to the 12th century. In the open market you can buy home-made bread, cheese and sausages, or even a bottle of patent medicine sold to you by an old-fashioned, slick-talking hawker. Antiques collectors will find many possibilities here, including religious statues and rustic furniture, as well as ordinary 19th-century household appliances.

it resembles a tropical rainforest. In 1511, Manuel I had a monastery built on this site. It was mostly destroyed in the earthquake of 1755, though a notable chapel and cloister survive. The present building is a bizarre and extravagant cocktail of Gothic, Renaissance, Manueline and Moorish architecture, fashioned as a love nest for Maria II (1834–53) and her smitten husband, Ferdinand of Saxe-Coburg-Gotha. Few have had the wealth to indulge their free-running fantasies so grandly. Like a child's dream castle, the exterior is a wild, layered construction painted pink, yellow, grey and red, with crenellated turrets, a studded archway and monsters guarding doorways. Inside, rooms are full of imaginative, ornate and, in some cases, suffocatingly sumptuous details. The views from the Disney-esque terraces of the platforms sweep all the way from the Atlantic to Lisbon.

Inside Mafra's church

Also located in and around Sintra are: the **Quinta da Regaleira**, a fantastic late 19th-century turreted mansion, with magical gardens speckled with follies such as the 'initiation well', which you can walk into down a spiralling staircase; the **Montserrate Palace Gardens**, wild, lush, and ideal for hiking; the **Palácio de Seteais**, an 18th-century palace that today is Sintra's fanciest hotel, and Sintra's excellent **Museum of Modern Art**. A short hop from Sintra

The fantastical Palácio da Pena

are the attractive village of **Colares** and the beach at **Praia das Maçãs**. Sintra's helpful tourist information office, on Praça da República in the old quarter, can direct you to any of these.

MAFRA AND ERICEIRA

The **Palácio Nacional de Mafra** ③ (www.palaciomafra.gov.pt; Wed–Mon 9.30am–5.30pm) at Mafra, is 40km (25 miles) to the northwest of Lisbon, and can be reached by bus from the terminal outside Campo Grande Metro station. In modest Portugal, the dimensions of this convent and palace are quite staggering. The frontage of the building, often likened to Spain's Escorial, measures over 220m (726ft). Mafra is so enormous that it is clearly visible from Sintra, approximately 16km (10 miles) away.

This monumental extravagance is attributable to João V, who in 1711 conceived this project to celebrate the long-awaited birth of his first child, Princess Dona Maria, after three years of marriage. A few statistics show the colossal scale of the project: 5,200 doorways, 2,500 windows and a 50,000-strong army of artists, artisans and labourers. A single carillon of 50 bells cost a shipload of gold. 'So cheap?' the king is said to have exclaimed. 'I'll take two.'

Your visit to the monastery-palace will take you from the apartments of João V at one end of the structure to the queen's apartments at the other end. The convent **library** is the undisputed highlight; it has a vaulted ceiling, a precious wood floor and tall shelves housing 30,000 books, making it the largest one-room library in Portugal. The **hospital** is a church with 16 private sickrooms lining the nave, so that patients could hear mass from their beds.

At Mafra is the church of Santo André, where Pedro Hispano was a priest before becoming Pope John XI in 1276, He remains Portugal's only pope.

Another 10km (6 miles) towards the coast is the fishing village and growing resort of **Ericeira** ㉜. The old section is a winsome town of cobbled streets winding between whitewashed cottages, with everything clean, neat and treasured by inhabitants and visitors alike. Ericeira received its town charter around 750 years ago, but scarcely attracted any attention until 1910, when Portugal's last king, Manuel II, hastily arrived from Mafra, and in its little port, boarded the royal yacht with his family to sail off into exile.

ESTORIL COAST

The Costa do Estoril (formerly called Costa do Sol) begins just west of Lisbon and goes all the way around the tip of the peninsula to Guincho on the open Atlantic. Those seeking pollution-free swimming (see page 92) usually head for Guincho, but the famous old resort of **Estoril** ㉝ itself, some 24km (15 miles) from Lisbon, is still worth a visit.

The half-hour train journey from Cais do Sodré station in Lisbon to Estoril goes through former fishing villages now turned into soulless commuter suburbs. If you go by the motorway (toll road) you will see nothing of them at all, but the coastal road still provides a scenic drive.

The railway station at Estoril is right alongside the beach. On the other side of the tracks (and across the coast road) is a formal park, the front lawn of the town's glitzy casino. With its nightclub, restaurants, bars, cinema, exhibition halls, shops and gaming rooms, this is Estoril's one-stop, after-dark amusement centre. In spite of the modern decor, the casino maintains an old-fashioned pace. Gambling is suspended only two nights a year: Good Friday and Christmas Eve. Legend has it that somebody broke the bank one Good Friday, prompting a superstitious management to declare it a holiday thenceforth. (Officials dismiss the story as wishful thinking.)

On the seafront at Cascais

The rest of Estoril is about as discreet as a Las Vegas high roller. Victorian villas and sleek modern mansions are tucked away behind green curtains of palms, eucalyptus, pines and vines. In the first half of the 20th century, dignitaries and monarchs, either unexpectedly unemployed or exiled, gravitated to Estoril or Cascais and luxurious hideaways.

As early as the mid-18th century, Estoril was attracting visitors because of its warm climate and thermal spa baths, which were considered good for liver complaints. It was a hangout for exiles and spies taking advantage of Portugal's neutrality during World War II, and Ian Fleming was inspired to write *Casino Royale* after his stay here. Long before that, however, prehistoric settlers had dug cave-cemeteries out of the limestone near the beach, discovered in 1944.

Cascais

Nearby **Cascais** ㉞, which sits on a pretty curved bay, lives a double life. It is a town of both fishermen and kings, where the humble and the retiring rich coexist with camera-toting visitors. The workaday fishing scene attracts tourists, who inspect the catch as it is unloaded from boats into wooden trays and then rushed to the modern auction building. There the fish are sold by a reverse (Dutch) auction, in which the price starts high and decreases until somebody shouts a bid. You may not understand the auctioneer's chant, but you'll see what he's selling: lobster, shrimp, hake, squid and sardines. Retail sales are in the hands of local fishwives, who set up stalls outside the market. For the finished product, try any of the dozen restaurants within walking distance of the beach.

Cascais' main square is charming, with swirling-patterned monochrome paving underfoot. The **Paços do Concelho** (Town Hall) has stately windows with iron railings, separated by panels of *azulejos* depicting saints. The fire station occupies a place of honour between the town hall and an attractive church, while in the square itself, stands a statue of Pedro I.

The sturdy-looking 17th-century fort, the **Cidadela** (Citadel), now occupied by the military, is one of the few buildings to have survived the earthquake and tidal wave of 1755. A chapel within the walls contains an image of St Anthony, traditionally carried on the back of a white mule in the parade on the feast day of Santo António (13 June).

After an overdose of sun and salt, the municipal park down the road is a cool relief. The palace in this park is a lovely villa housing the **Museu dos Condes de Castro Guimarães** (Museum of the Counts of Castro Guimarães; Rua Júlio Pereira de Mello; www.cascais.pt/equipamento/museu-condes-de-

The main square of Cascais

castro-guimaraes; Tue–Sun 10am–1pm, 2–5pm), a museum with archaeological remains, artworks, old furniture, gold and silver. For a more complete picture of the resort's fishing heritage and royal connections, visit the intriguing **Museu do Mar – Rei Dom Carlos** (King Carlos Museum of the Seas; www.cascais.pt/equipa mento/museu-do-mar-rei-d-carlos; Tue–Fri 10am–5pm, Sat–Sun 10am–1pm and 2–5pm; free), which has historic photographs of the king, who was an enthusiastic marine biologist, at leisure, as well as the costumes and customs of the fisherfolk.

The road out of Cascais to the west passes **Boca do Inferno** (Mouth of Hell), a geological curiosity where, in rough weather, the waves send up astonishingly high spouts of spray accompanied by ferocious sound effects. On a day when the sea is calm, you'll wonder what all the fuss is about.

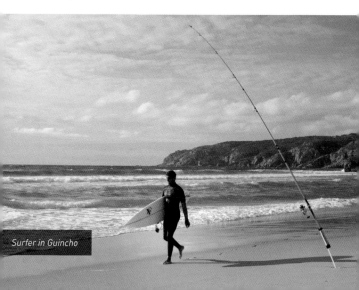

Surfer in Guincho

Cabo da Roca

At **Guincho**, you have the choice of either a sandy beach or the rocks to fish from, but be careful – they face the open sea and it's often rough, and hence a windsurfer's heaven. Just up the coast you can see the windswept cape of **Cabo da Roca,** the most westerly point of mainland Europe. You can reach the cape by continuing on from Guincho, through Malveira, and then turning left. A

Boca do Inferno

right turn at the same points leads you along a winding road through the glorious, pine-scented **Serra de Sintra**, finishing up back in Sintra (see page 66).

SOUTH OF LISBON

Sesimbra

It's around 32km (20 miles) south from Lisbon over the bridge to the calm, clean seashore at **Sesimbra** ㉟. The beach, the main draw for the mostly Portuguese crowd that gathers here at weekends and holidays, not least for its splendid seafood restaurants, is narrow but long, and is sheltered from the brunt of Atlantic tides and harsh winds. Sesimbra is an important fishing centre, and most of the local adult male population seems to be involved in the industry. Fishing boats set out from the **harbour** at the far,

Busy beach at Sesimbra

western end of the town, to bring home their catches of sardine, horse mackerel, hake and swordfish.

Largo 5 de Outubro is a small square in the centre of town, where locals sit and gossip under a giant floral canopy of bougainvillea. Adjacent is the **Misericórdia Church**, with its upturned keel roof. Founded during the 15th century, it contains the much-venerated image of Senhor Jesus das Chagas, the patron of the Sesimbra fishing community, and a painting of Nossa Senhora da Misericórdia.

The **castle walls** silhouetted on the hilltop above Sesimbra are the genuine article, though restored. During the Middle Ages the whole town was up there, protected against sea raiders by the walls and the altitude. The Moors built the enclave, lost it to Dom Afonso Henriques in 1165, and won it back again for a few years before having to move out permanently in 1200. Within the outer fortifications is the Church of Our Lady of the

Consolation of the Castle, destroyed during the 12th century and rebuilt during the 18th. Take a peek inside: the walls are covered with *azulejos* from floor to ceiling. The castle is open daily and free to visitors. The view down to the curve of the coast and back to the Arrábida mountains is magnificent.

Serra da Arrábida

The topographical highlight of the Arrábida peninsula is the **Serra da Arrábida**, a mountain chain approximately 35km (22 miles) long that protects the coast from the strong north winds and accounts for the Mediterranean vegetation. In the west the peninsula ends with the dramatic cliffs of **Cabo Espichel**.

The 12km (7.5-mile) route across the Serra is winding and narrow, but it provides an attractive introduction to the wonderfully rugged **Parque Natural da Arrábida** , which covers more than 10,000 hectares (24,700 acres). From the surface of the sea the Serra rises a sheer 500m (1,650ft). Science describes this rolling heathland as a glacial relict, its primitive forests preserved when glaciers melted.

Wild slopes contrast with the intense blue of the sea below; come in spring and the park is bright with wild flowers. The old monastery nestled in the hills has been

Fresh catch on the coast

resurrected as part of Lisbon University. Down below, on the coast, the little beach spot of **Portinho da Arrábida** is popular with Portuguese weekenders.

Setúbal

Setúbal ③, the district capital, is a 20-minute drive from Lisbon by motorway, longer if you take the picturesque route via Sesimbra and Arrábida. (The bus does it in an hour; or you can take the 30-minute ferry across the Tagus and then a 45-minute train ride.) This is olive and citrus country, with cows grazing among the trees. The further south you go, the more significant the vineyards; the Setúbal region produces a highly regarded Muscatel.

Setúbal is a conglomeration of market town, industrial centre and resort, and is Portugal's third-largest fishing port. Narrow,

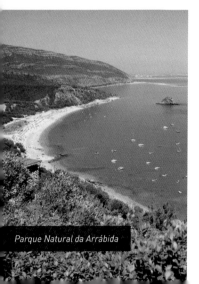

Parque Natural da Arrábida

inviting shopping streets twist through the centre of the city. Its greatest historical and artistic treasure, the Gothic **Igreja de Jesus** (currently undergoing restoration), was built around 1490 by the great French architect Diogo Boitac, who later built Lisbon's glorious Jerónimos Monastery (see page 51).

The adjoining monastery has been converted into the **Museu de Cidade** (Tue–Sat 10am–6pm, Sun summer 4–6pm, winter 3–7pm) with a mixture

Barrels stored at a winery in Setúbal

of early Portuguese paintings, including a series of the life of Jesus, archaeological odds and ends, antique furniture and tiles. Part of the collection is dedicated to the Portuguese Romantic poet, Manuel Maria Barbosa du Bocage. The cloister was reconstructed after the 1755 earthquake, but since then excavation has revealed parts of the original patio. Part of the museum exposition has been moved to **Galeria Municipal do Banco de Portugal** (Tue–Fri 11am–2pm and 3–6pm, Sat 11am–1pm and 2–6pm, Sun 2–6pm). Some exhibits including books from the Museu de Cidade can also be seen at **Casa Bocage** (Tue–Fri 9am–12.30pm and 2–5.30pm, Sat summer 3–7pm, winter 2–6pm).

The 16th-century star-shaped fort, high above the town to the west, is now a government-sponsored *pousada* with great views (see page 141). Some action is usually taking place down in the fishermen's quarter when brightly painted boats of all sizes return with their freshly caught fish.

Easter procession

WHAT TO DO

SHOPPING

Many of Lisbon's shops seem not to have changed in style for at least 100 years, and have an appealing old-fashioned aesthetic, while in the narrow streets of Bairro Alto, young designers show off their latest creations and have DJs playing while you browse. Here you can buy handicrafts, notably ceramics, which have been produced in the same way for hundreds of years. There are also chic boutiques, glittering malls and a wonderfully scruffy outdoor market.

BEST BUYS

Handicrafts excel in Portugal. *Azulejos*, the hand-painted ceramic tiles that have been decorating Portugal's walls throughout the centuries, are one of the top crafts. You can buy a scene on a single blue-and-white tile, an address plaque for your house or a batch to assemble into a picture when you get home. Some shops will paint tiles to order if you have a particular design in mind, and some will copy a photograph.

Delicate Portuguese **embroidery** and **lacework**, especially samples by women on the island of Madeira, is excellent. Hand-embroidered goods, such as tablecloths, napkins and hand towels, also come from the Azores and some mainland towns, notably Viana do Castelo.

Shopping card

The Lisboa Eat and Shop Card offers discounts of up to 15 percent in Baixa, Chiado and Av. Liberdade. The card is available in one- and two-day versions from Turismo de Lisboa offices.

Hand-painted cockerels

Filigree work is of very high quality. Look for silver filigree earrings and delicate brooches, often in the form of flowers or butterflies. Portuguese **pottery** and **ceramics** are found in many designs and colours, from fine porcelain **Vista Alegre** to folksy earthenware. Hand-painted brightly coloured **cockerels** from Barcelos are the ubiquitous national symbol.

Arraiolos, an Alentejo village, has been making fine **wool rugs** in bright colours and graceful designs for centuries. **Hand-woven baskets**, which differ by region, are strong, utilitarian and often pretty. Artefacts made from **cork** are typical; Portugal is the world's leading producer, not only for wine bottles, but also for umbrellas and bags.

Portugal has long been famous for its fortified **port wine** from the Douro Valley near Oporto in the north. Best known as an after-dinner tradition, it also comes in aperitif versions (see page 104). Vintage port from the most select years is what connoisseurs and collectors seek, but there are more accessible ports to take home. Look for aged tawny, LBV (late bottle vintages) or, for something a little more unusual, a bottle of white port.

Madeira wine, from the volcanic soil of the Portuguese island in the Atlantic, is served either before dinner or afterwards as a dessert wine. While these regional wines get much of the attention, Portugal also produces a number of excellent red and white table wines. Look for those from Dão and Alentejo, as well as *vinhos verdes* (young wines) from the Minho.

To enjoy the sounds of Portugal back home, take home a classic ***fado* recording**, perhaps by the late Amália Rodrigues or by Carlos Paredes.

A number of **high-fashion designers** from Portugal – such as Ana Salazar and Fátima Lopes – have gained international attention, and Chiado and Bairro Alto are good places to seek them out. Hand-knitted pullovers in sophisticated designs or chunky fishermen's sweaters from Nazaré are good buys.

The Portuguese leather industry is known throughout the world and jackets, belts, bags, wallets and shoes are popular and good-value buys.

WHERE TO SHOP

Most city shops are open Monday to Friday from 9 or 10am to 7pm (smaller ones might take a lunch break, usually between 1 and 3pm); the more traditional shops close on Saturday at 1pm. Modern shopping malls are usually open from 10am to midnight or later, and sometimes on Sunday.

The **Chiado** district is the place to go for books, smart designer wear and interior design, especially the **Armazéns do Chiado** mall (www.armazensdo

Haberdasher's facade in Baixa

chiado.com) and Rua Garrett. The French-owned Fnac department store here is popular.

The central grid of streets around Rua Augusta in the **Baixa** contains wonderfully atmospheric shops, sustained by low rents. Traditional foodstuffs, clothing and jewellery are all sold here.

Across the street from Cais de Sodre station is the renovated, 19th-century **Mercado da Ribeira** (Sun–Wed 10pm–midnight; Thur–Sat 10pm–2am), which houses a daily food market, full of colourful produce, and selling everything from piri-piri sauce to formal flower arrangements. At night the market becomes a foodies' paradise with dozens of food stalls representing the best restaurants in Lisbon. Tasting menus are great value and the place has already become one of the favourite meeting points for locals and tourists alike. Markets are fun for their ambience as much as the goods on offer. Behind São Vicente de Fora church, in the Campo de Santa Clara, the **Feira da Ladra** ('Thieves' Market') is held on Tuesday and Saturday from 9am to 6pm. On the fringes of the kitchenware and clothing stalls are dusty treasures and an incredible range of second-hand items.

Lisbon has two main shopping centres. **Amoreiras** (Avenida Engenheiro Duarte Pacheco; www.amoreiras.com) is a pastel-coloured complex laid out over three floors. It houses banks, a post office, cinemas, a health club, supermarkets, a chapel, art galleries, eating places and over 200 shops selling goods from furniture and linen to music, books, china and chocolate. **Centro Columbo** (Avenida Lusiada, Benfica; www.colombo.pt) is the city's largest shopping centre, more akin to a massive leisure complex than a mere shopping mall. Come here for all the major chains, plus a nursery, chapel, cinema, health club, golf driving range, bowling alley and funfair. Alternatively, head for the largest branch of the Spanish chain **El Corte Ingles** (Avenida Antonio Augusto Aguiar, 31; www.elcorteingles.pt) or **Atrium**

Local produce in Mercado da Ribeira

Saldanha (Praça Duque de Saldanha; www.atriumsaldanha.pt), with a great variety of snack and light meal options.

Out near Cascais, beside the motorway, **CascaiShopping** (www.cascaishopping.pt) is another shopping complex. For easy shopping closer to town, you might like to try the **Centro Commercial de Alvalade** (www.ccalvalade.pt) and the fashionable but generally expensive **Avenida da Roma**.

ENTERTAINMENT

The Portuguese capital is a great place to party, with venues ranging from *fado* speakeasies to superclubs, and from African nightclubs to alternative bars, clustered in various areas around the city.

Nightclubs, bars and live music. The classic nighttime outing in Lisbon is still to the *fado* houses in Alfama or Bairro Alto.

A century ago, 'respectable' people were reluctant to be seen in a *fado* club; nowadays the danger is not to your reputation, only to your wallet, as tickets and drinks are quite expensive. Many offer dinner as well as drinks.

Good *fado* clubs include Senhor Vinho (Rua do Meio à Lapa 18; tel: 213-972 681; www.srvinho.com), Alfama's A Baîuca (Rua de São Miguel 20; tel: 218-867 284), a low-key local place, and Fado in Chiado (Espaço Chiado, Rua da Misericordia 14; tel: 961 717 778; www.fadoinchiado.com).

Nightlife areas are clustered around dock areas, and these venues tend towards a more mainstream crowd, but the biggest buzz is to be found in Bairro Alto, where there are nightclubs, jazz clubs and bars for all tastes, some open until 5am.

Eclectic bars include gay-friendly Portas Largas (Rua da Atalaia 105) and the jazz-centred Café Tati (R. da Ribeira Nova

⊙ FADO

Fado, the soulful Portuguese song – literally 'fate', translated into music – is based on a story or poem and accompanied by a 12-string guitar. The dramatic atmosphere of a *fado* house adds to the occasion. Guitarists start off the proceedings with a warm-up number. The lights dim, the audience goes quiet, and a spotlight picks out a woman in black who begins to wail out a song of tragedy and despair. Her sultry voice sums up that most Portuguese emotion, *saudade* – a swell of longing, regret and nostalgia. Though most often characterised by melancholy or despair, there are also joyful and relatively upbeat *fados*.

Most *fado* singers are women, but you are also likely to hear a man perform the same sort of ballad with a strong, husky voice.

Fado performers

36), which has regular live music. North of Bairro Alto, the area around Principe Real is the centre of the city's gay scene and also home to the fantastical bar, Pavilhão Chinês (Rua Dom Pedro V 89-91), worth a visit for a cocktail amid its extraordinary crazy-attic, clutter-lined decor.

The club to visit in Lisbon is riverside Lux (Avenida Infante Dom Henrique; www.luxfragil.com), which is run by nightlife guru Marcel Reis. It's enduringly chic, edgy and interesting, despite being a super-club.

Concerts and dance. Lisbon's cultural scene offers occasional opera, symphony concerts, ballet and recitals, usually held in winter. The city's opera company is well regarded, and the Gulbenkian Foundation (see page 57) maintains its own symphony orchestra and choir company.

Portugal has three other important symphony orchestras and a national dance company.

Venues include: Coliseu dos Recreios (Rua das Portas de Santo Antão 96; tel: 213-240 580, www.coliseulisboa.com), the second-largest music and events hall in Lisbon; Altice Arena (Parque das Nações; tel: 218-918 409, http://arena.altice.pt), the place for big-time rock bands and Brazilian acts; Museu Gulbenkian (Avenida de Berna 45; tel: 217-823 000, www.gulbenkian.pt), which hosts varied recitals, classical music and dance programmes, including open-air concerts in summer; Teatro Nacional de São Carlos (Rua Serpa Pinto 9; tel: 213-253 000, http://tnsc.pt/), Lisbon's opera house; and Centro Cultural de Belém (Praça do Império; tel: 213-612 400, www.ccb.pt), which has a wide programme of cultural performances.

Theatre and cinema. Most of Lisbon's stage plays are comedies and revues – in Portuguese, of course. The best-known theatre is **Teatro Nacional de Dona Maria II** (Praça de Dom Pedro IV, Rossio; tel: 213-250 800, www.tndm.pt).

Canoes lined up at Praia dos Pescadores, Cascais

Cinemas tend to show foreign films in the original language with Portuguese subtitles. **São Jorge** (Avenida Liberdade 175; tel: 213-103 400, www.cinemasaojorge.pt) is a pleasantly renovated cinema with three screens, and often hosts festivals.

Gambling. The **Estoril Casino** (tel: 214-667 700, www.casino-estoril.pt; see page 73) is the big draw for gamblers. To enter the gaming rooms you have to pay a fee and show your passport. The casino is open daily 3pm–3am (closed Christmas Eve). A sign suggests that gentlemen wear jackets after 8pm, but no rules are enforced.

SPORTS

From swimming and hiking to deep-sea fishing, sports enthusiasts have plenty of options in the Lisbon area. The temperate climate also means year-round golf and tennis. If you're interested in diving or water skiing, or any other sport for which you need to hire equipment, ask at the tourist information offices in each town about the best places to do so.

ACTIVE SPORTS

Diving. Just off Sesimbra, south of Lisbon, the clear, calm waters are very good for snorkelling and scuba diving.

Fishing. All along the coast you will see anglers in boots casting off from the beaches, and others perched on rocks or man-made promontories. The best deep-sea fishing is for swordfish around the coast of Sesimbra (contact Marlin Boat Tours; http://marlintours.com/).

Golf. The Lisbon and Tagus Valley area has 18 courses, including top-rated Estoril Golf Club (18 holes; tel: 214-680 176), one of the oldest in the country, at Estoril; Estoril Sol Academia (9 holes; tel: 219-240 331) near Sintra; Lisbon Sports Club (18 holes; tel: 214-310 077) at Belas near Queluz; and Quinta da Marinha (18 holes; tel: 214-860 100; www.quintadamarinha.com) near Cascais, designed by Robert Trent Jones.

Riding. You can hire a horse, with or without an instructor, at the Clube Equestre de Janas (Rua do Alecrim, s/n, Sintra) or at the Quinta da Marinha, which also has an equestrian centre.

Day trip to the beach

Sailing and boating. Most beaches protected from the open ocean have rowing boats, canoes or pedalos for rent by the hour. Experienced sailors in search of a more seaworthy craft should ask at the local yacht marina. Rowing boats are also available at Parque das Nações near the Oceanário.

Swimming. Because of pollution along the Estoril Coast, you should not swim in the sea any closer to Lisbon than at Estoril itself, which has been granted an EU blue flag. At Guincho and beyond, the sea is perfectly clean and quite safe for swimming, but beware of the strong undertow. South of Lisbon from Caparica onwards is delightful, but can also be windy, with very rough seas.

Tennis. Major hotels tend to have their own tennis courts, but there are tennis clubs and public courts as well. Many golf clubs also have tennis courts.

SPECTATOR SPORTS

Bullfights. Portuguese bullfighting follows a style called *Arte Marialva*. Unlike Spanish bullfights, the bull – its horns sheathed – is not killed. There's artistry in the partnership between the splendidly dressed *cavaleiro* and his horse but, as barbed darts are planted into the bull's upper back, bullfighting remains a bloody spectacle. The horseman is aided by a back-up team, *peões de brega*, with distracting capes. They are succeeded in the arena by an eight-man team of volunteer *forcados*, wearing tight breeches, white stockings and short coat, who face the bull barehanded. All performers are judged on skill, style and courage. At the end the bull is led away among farm steers and is afterwards butchered.

Lisbon's **Campo Pequeno Praça de Touros** bullring (tel: 217- 998 450, www.campopequeno.com), at the top of Avenida da República, is a Victorian red-brick landmark with mock-Moorish arches and bulbous domes. The season runs from Easter Sunday to October. As in Spain, seats in the shade *(sombra)* cost more than in the sun *(sol)*. For a modicum of comfort, rent a pillow from the usher.

Motor racing. Races and events take place at Estoril's Autodrome.

Football (Soccer). Football draws big crowds in Portugal. Lisbon's two major teams are Benfica, which plays at the Estádio da Luz, and Sporting Clube de Portugal, which holds matches at Estádio do José Alvalade near Campo Grande.

CHILDREN'S ACTIVITIES

With its trams, elevators, funiculars, ferries and tourist trains, Lisbon offers

Football flags flying at Benfica

some great ways to entertain children just by touring around the city. Take the Transtejo ferry to Belém or the **Parque das Nações**, which has a splendid aquarium (Oceanário de Lisboa, see page 61), playgrounds, fountains, paddleboats and aerial cable cars. The **Planetário Calouste Gulbenkian** (http://ccm.marinha.pt/pt/planetario) in Belém (see page 53) has special planetarium shows for school children.

North of the aqueduct is **Jardim Zoológico de Lisboa** (Zoo, Estrada de Benfica 158-60; tel: 217-232 900/910; www.zoo.pt; daily 10am-6pm, until 8pm Apr-Sept;). There are elephant rides, boats and a miniature train, and shows at various times of day when animals from parrots to dolphins are fed. There is also **Tapada Nacional de Mafra**, a wildlife park with deer, wolves and wild boar at Mafra (www.tapadademafra.pt; daily 9.30am-6pm).

Giraffes at the zoo

Campo Grande, between the zoo and the airport, is a popular park. Palm, cedar and willow trees shade pretty walks, and there's a small lake with rowing boats.

For a safe beach with clean water you'll have to travel some way from the city (see page 92). Head for Guincho and Caparica when the wind is light, or Sesimbra and Tróia otherwise. Caparica has a water park with long, twisting slides.

CALENDAR OF EVENTS

As you plan your excursions, it is worth checking details of festivals and fairs in and around Lisbon with tourist information offices.

January–December Fado in Chiado. Live Fado shows held at the Teatro de Artes Cenicas in Chiado every evening (except Sundays) at 7pm.

February–March Carnival (Mardi Gras). Processions and fireworks.

March Moda Lisboa, Lisbon fashion week.

March–April Easter services and processions.

April Peixe em Lisboa food festival. Dias da Música em Belém, music festival at Centro Cultural de Belém. Estoril Open ATP/WTA tennis tournament.

May Pilgrimage to Fátima (12–13 May). IndieLisboa, Portugal's biggest independent film festival.

May–June Alkantara Art Festival. Rock in Rio (every two years), long-running rock festival featuring international stars.

May–September Bullfighting season at the Moorish-style Campo Pequeno in the north of the city.

June Festival of music, dance and theatre (all month). *Festas dos santos populares* (festivals of the popular saints) starting with St Anthony (13 June), on the eve of his feast day there's a costumed parade down the Avenida da Liberdade followed by celebrations in Alfama; the nights of St John (23 June) and St Peter (28 June) are almost as festive, and the season finishes with a burst of fireworks.

July Sintra music festival (second week), including live performances in the town's historic palaces and gardens.

July–August Estoril International Music Festival. Cool Jazz in Marquez de Pombal Gardens, Oeiras.

August Jazz em Agosto – jazz concerts at the Museu Gulbenkian. Cascais Sea Festival (Festas do Mar).

October Estoril Open Golf Tournament. DocLisboa documentary film festival.

November Arte Lisboa contemporary art fair. Dia de São Martinho (St Martin's Day), when the year's new wine is tasted.

EATING OUT

The Lisbon dining scene has become much more diverse in recent years. The Bairro Alto is still one of the best areas for eating out, and is dense with restaurants of all kinds, especially small traditional dives. But as Lisbon moves to embrace the river again, restaurants have been popping up along the old dock areas: Doca de Alcântara, Doca do Poço do Bispo and Doca Jardim do Tabaco – and along the riverfront near the Parque das Nações. Another popular eating area is the rejuvenated Mercado da Ribeira (see page 86).

Seafood is perhaps the best thing to try, as there is a surfeit of fresh fish and shellfish. Not that restaurants skimp on meat:

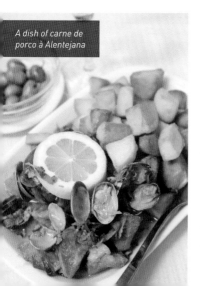

A dish of carne de porco à Alentejana

you can find delicious pork or lamb dishes and steak. More adventurous palates can try cuisines imported from Portugal's former African and Asian colonies.

Portions in Portuguese restaurants tend to be generous. You can ask for a half portion (which is usually charged at approximately two-thirds the full price).

Even the top restaurants in Lisbon are fairly affordable by the standards of European capitals. The 'tourist menu' (ementa turística) in many restaurants, particularly at lunchtime, can be an excellent value at 10–15 euros. It is an economically priced set meal – typically bread, butter, soup, main course and dessert, with wine, beer, mineral water or a soft drink included.

RESTAURANTS AND MENUS

Government inspectors rate all Portuguese restaurants in four categories or *classes*. In descending order the classes are: *luxo* (luxury), *primeira* (first), *segunda* (second) and *terceira* (third). The scale is also an indicator of how costly a meal is likely to be. A rating sign is often displayed outside restaurants, while menus shown in the window or beside the door let you know what to expect in variety and price. Prices normally include taxes and a service charge, but you are expected to leave an extra five to 10 percent tip for good service.

Whether you indulge in one of Lisbon's chic riverfront restaurants or absorb some local colour in a simple backstreet family-run place, you are likely to come across a variety of dishes and preparations entirely new to you.

The prices displayed outside some of Lisbon's cafés may apply only if you stand at the bar. In Portugal, as in some other European countries, if you sit down at a table, you will have to pay the higher prices quoted on the regular menu. Also, in restaurants where seafood portions are charged by

Free appetisers?

Most restaurants serve a *couvert* – unrequested appetisers such as cheese, ham and meat and fish pastes that appear to be free. They are not. You will be charged a few euros for these, but some, such as shellfish, can be much more expensive. If you do not touch them, you should not be charged for them. You may have to point this out; few people opt to abstain.

weight, waiters may bring out repeated portions without your specifically ordering more. If you don't refuse them early on, the bill might be quite a shock.

MEALTIMES

Breakfast *(pequeno almoço)* is usually eaten any time until about 10am. **Lunch** *(almoço)* is served from shortly after noon until 3pm, and **dinner** *(jantar)* runs from 7.30 to 9.30pm (or later in a *casa de fado*). Snacks between meals are usually taken at a *pastelaria* (pastry and cake shop), *salão de chá* (tea shop), or what the Portuguese call, in English, a *snack bar* – an over-the-counter bar, selling sandwiches, savoury pastries and sweets.

Because lunch and dinner tend to be major events, you may prefer the kind of light breakfast the Portuguese eat: coffee, toast or rolls, butter and jam. Larger hotels usually provide all the extras – such as juice, cereal, eggs and bacon.

SOUPS AND SEAFOOD

Soups. Lunch and dinner often get off to a solid start, and soups are hale-and-hearty typical Portuguese fare. *Caldo verde* (green soup) is a thick broth of potato purée with finely shredded cabbage or kale. Sometimes sausage is added. *Sopa à Portuguesa* is similar to *caldo verde*, but with added broccoli, turnips, beans, carrots and anything else the cook happens to have to hand.

Sopa de cozido is a rich meat broth with cabbage and perhaps macaroni added. (This course is often followed by *cozido*, a huge serving of all the things that were boiled to create the broth, including beef, chicken, pork,

Salt and pepper
Salt and pepper are seldom put on the table. However, you will be given them if you ask: *Sal e pimenta, faz favor*.

sausages, potatoes, cabbage and carrots.) *Canja de galinha* is simple chicken-and-rice soup.

Seafood. The best advertisement for seafood is usually the window of a restaurant: a generous refrigerated display case with crabs and prawns, oysters and mussels, sea bass and sole. Seafood restaurants generally sell shellfish by the weight, giving the price in euros per kilo. The Portuguese

Seafood is in abundance

are very fond of boiled and grilled fish dishes, usually served with generous portions of cabbage and boiled potatoes and doused with a little oil and vinegar.

A number of seafood dishes are true local specialities. *Caldeirada* is a rich seafood stew. *Amêijoas na cataplana* is an invention from the Algarve, of steamed clams (or mussels) with sausages, tomato, white wine, ham, onion and herbs. *Açorda de marisco* is a spicy, garlic-scented thick bread soup full of seafood bits; raw eggs are later added to the mixture. *Lulas recheadas* are squid stuffed with rice, olives, tomato, onion and herbs, though large squid (*chocos*) are often simply grilled. *Lampreia à Minho* is lamprey, not always highly regarded, but quite a delicacy in Portugal, served with a bed of rice and red wine sauce (best from January to March).

Sardinhas (sardines) are excellent in Lisbon and are often served charcoal-grilled (*sardinhas assadas*).

Bacalhau (cod) is the national dish of Portugal, even though it can be expensive nowadays, and comes dried and salted, and from distant seas. The Portuguese say that cod is served in 100, 365 or 1,000 different ways, depending on the teller's taste for hyperbole. One of the best ways to try it is in *Bacalhau à Gomes de Sá*, in which flaky chunks are baked with parsley, potatoes, onion and olives and garnished with crumbled hard-boiled egg. Fresh fish, whole or filleted, is usually served grilled, as are *atum* (tuna) and *espadarte* (swordfish steaks). For those who know some Spanish or Portuguese, *peixe espada* might sound like swordfish but is actually scabbard fish, a long, thin fish that comes from the area south of Lisbon.

MEAT AND GAME

Bife na frigideira is not what you might think. *Frigideira* means frying pan, and this dish is beefsteak cooked in a wine sauce. *Cabrito assado* is baked kid served with rice and potato, heavy going but delicious. *Carne de porco à Alentejana* is an inspired dish of clams and pork cooked with paprika and garlic. *Espetada mista* means Portuguese shish kebab: chunks of beef, lamb and pork on a spit. *Feijoada* is the national dish of Brazil, the former Portuguese colony. In Portugal, it's not nearly as elaborate or ritualised, but it's still a hearty and tasty stew of pigs' feet and sausage, white beans and cabbage.

Frango (chicken) is popular and prepared many ways: stewed in wine sauce, fried, roasted and barbecued to a tasty crisp. Some restaurants specialise in game

Market price

If you see *'preço V* (or simply *'PV'*) beside the seafood or shellfish on a menu, it means that the price is variable depending on the day's market price. Ask the price before ordering.

– *codorniz* (quail), *perdiz* (partridge), *lebre* (hare) and even *javali* (wild boar).

DESSERT AND CHEESE

The Portuguese have a sweet tooth. Portuguese cakes, custards and pastries made with egg yolks and sugar are delicious, especially the *pastéis de nata* (custard tarts). *Pudim flan* is the Portuguese version of crème caramel; it has many variations, including *Pudim de Marfim*. *Arroz*

Custard tarts from Belém

doce is rice pudding with a dash of cinnamon. *Maçã assada* is a tasty sugary baked apple. *Pudim Molotov* sounds like a bomb, and indeed it's so rich that it's sure to explode any strict diet – the fluffy egg-white mousse is immersed in a sticky caramel sauce.

And then there's cheese. The richest and most expensive in Portugal is *Serra da Estrela*, a delicious cured ewe's-milk cheese that originates high up in the mountains. Also on many menus is *Flamengo*, a mild cheese very similar to Edam. Some restaurants serve *queijo fresco* as an appetiser. This is a small, white, soft mini-cheese made of ewe's and goat's milk, but it's fairly bland, so you may want to season it with pepper and salt.

INTERNATIONAL AND EXOTIC CUISINE

Portugal's cuisine is infused with tastes from other cultures, an advantage of its colonial baggage, which means that you can experiment with different cuisines while you're in Lisbon. The former colony of Goa accounts for the local popularity of *caril* (curry) and other Indian-style dishes. A typical Goan delicacy, a lot less pungent than Indian food, is *xacuti* (pronounced and some-times spelled *chacuti*). The dish is simply chunks of fried chicken in a sauce of pepper, coriander, saffron, cinnamon, cumin, anise, cloves and coconut milk served with steamed rice. *Piri-piri* is a hot-pepper condiment and preparation from Angola that will set most mouths ablaze. Order a *piri-piri* dish with extreme caution.

Four centuries of ties with the territory of Macau assures all lovers of Chinese food a night out with dishes such as *gambas doces* (sweet-and-sour prawns).

TABLE WINES

Portuguese wines are generally good, and several regions pro-duce truly excellent wines. Ask the waiter for *tinto* (red) or *branco* (white). *Vinho verde* (green wine), produced in the northwest, is like a young white wine, but fizzy, light and delightful. A lesser-known type is a red wine from the same region, bearing the seemingly oxymoronic name *vinho verde tinto* (red green wine).

Both of these wines should be served chilled, as should Portuguese rosé, which is also slightly bubbly, and may be either sweet or very dry. *Vinhos maduros* are mature, or aged, wines.

Vinho espumante is Portuguese sparkling wine, packaged in a Champagne-shaped bottle. Most are sweet, but you can also find some quite dry versions.

Vintage port

A bottle of vintage port should be consumed within 48 hours of opening. At home or in Portugal, don't pay a high price for a glass of a rare vintage port unless the bartender or waiter opens the bottle in front of you. For most establishments, that's too expensive a proposition.

All of the best wine-producing regions have names whose use is controlled by law *(região demarcada)*. You may come across these classifications: Bucelas, a light and fresh white wine; Colares, a traditional red wine; and Setúbal, a mellow, sweet white, sometimes served as an aperitif. Dão and Douro in the north produce vigorous reds and flavourful whites. Wines from the Alentejo region are also highly regarded.

Barrels at a winery

The two most celebrated Portuguese wines, port and Madeira, are mostly known as dessert wines, but may also be sipped as aperitifs. The before-dinner varieties are dry or extra-dry white port and the dry Madeiras, *Sercial* and *Verdelho*. These should be served slightly chilled. After dinner, sip one of the famous tawny ports (the aged varieties are especially good), or a Madeira dessert wine, *Boal* or *Malvasia* (malmsey).

OTHER DRINKS

Portuguese beers are good and refreshing. Light or dark, they are served chilled, bottled or from the tap. One of the best and most common brands is Sagres. *Aguardente* (literally 'fire water') is the local brandy. *Aguardente velha* (old) is a fine digestif.

Coffee is the main choice of beverage during the day and at the end of lunch or dinner. Most people order a *bica*, a small cup of black espresso coffee – also called simply *um café* or *um café espresso*.

Tea (*chá*, pronounced 'shah'), by the bag, is also drunk – after all, it was the Portuguese explorers who first introduced it to the rest of the Western world. Although the concept of afternoon tea is generally regarded as British, its origins are in fact Portuguese, dating from 1662, when Catherine of Bragança, sister of Dom Afonso VI, married the English King Charles II. Her fashionable court popularised tea drinking.

⊙ PORT AND MADEIRA

Thanks to the unique growing conditions of the Douro Valley in the north of Portugal, fortified port wine has tantalised palates around the world since the British began exporting it in the 17th century. It differs from other wines due to the microclimate and soil of the region, and to the fact that the fermentation process is stopped with brandy. Around 10 percent of the grapes picked each year are still crushed in treading rooms by barefoot men. After two or three days' fermentation the brandy is added. The following spring, the fortified wine is sent to mature at the lodges on the banks of the River Douro at Vila Nova de Gaia (opposite Porto), from where it is shipped.

First produced on the island of Madeira in the 15th century, Madeira wine became an important export trade due to a combination of its notable quality and Madeira's position on the shipping lanes to the Indies. With the rise of the British colonies in North America and the West Indies, it fast became a favourite on both sides of the Atlantic. Madeira wine only became a fortified wine when, like port, it was decided to add grape brandy to stabilise it on long sea voyages.

TO HELP YOU ORDER...

Could we have a table? **Queremos uma mesa?**
Do you have a set-price menu? **Tem uma ementa turística?**
I'd like a/an/some... **Queria...**

beer **uma cerveja**	napkin **guardanapo**
the bill a **conta**	pepper **pimenta**
bread **pão**	potatoes **batatas**
butter **manteiga**	salad **salada**
dessert **sobremesa**	salt **sal**
fish **peixe**	sandwich **sanduíche**
fruit **fruta**	soup **sopa**
ice-cream **gelado**	sugar **açúcar**
meat **carne**	tea **chá**
the menu **a carta**	vegetables **legumes**
milk **leite**	wine **vinho**
mineral water **água mineral**	wine list **carta de vinos**

MENU READER

alho garlic	**lombo** fillet
amêijoas baby clams	**lulas** squid
arroz rice	**mariscos** shellfish
assado roast, baked	**mexilhões** mussels
bacalhau cod	**ostras** oysters
besugo sea bream	**ovo** egg
dobrada tripe	**pescada** hake
dourada sea bass	**pescadinha** whiting
feijões beans	**polvos** baby octopus
frito fried	**queijo** cheese
gambas prawns	**salmonete** red mullet
lagosta spiny lobster	**truta** trout
lenguado sole	**vitela** veal

PLACES TO EAT

The prices indicated here are for dinner with starter, main course and dessert, with wine, per person. (Note that some fish or shellfish dishes will be more expensive.) Tax (IVA) is included. All restaurants listed here accept major credit cards. Note that many Lisbon restaurants close for the entire month of August.

€€€€	over 45 euros
€€€	30–45 euros
€€	20–30 euros
€	below 20 euros

LISBON

Alfama

A Baiuca €€€ *Rua de São Miguel 20, tel: 218-867 284*. Open for dinner, closed Tue. This small, family-run Alfama restaurant offers good Portuguese fare and amateur fado performances (Thu–Mon).

Casa do Leão €€€€ *Castelo de São Jorge, tel: 218-875 962,* www.pousadas.pt. Open daily for lunch and dinner daily. The only restaurant inside the castle ramparts serves a wide range of traditional Portuguese and international dishes, with excellent views.

Chapitô á Mesa €€€ *Costa do Castelo 7, tel: 218-875 077*, http://chapito.org. Open daily for lunch and dinner. This restaurant serves up hearty Portuguese food, and offers stunning views over the city.

Bairro Alto

100 Maneiras €€€€ *Rua do Teixeira 35, tel: 910-918 181,* www.restaurante100maneiras.com . Open daily for dinner only. An intimate, elegant restaurant that is foodie heaven, offering a very reasonably priced 10-course tasting menu (€100 including wines); each dish is a surprise. Chef Ljubomir Stanisic also has a less formal and cheaper bistro at 9 Largo de Trinidade in Chiado.

Cervejaria da Trindade €€ *Rua Nova da Trindade 20, tel: 213-423 506,* www.cervejariatrindade.pt. Open daily for lunch and dinner (until late). A famous old beer hall and restaurant, in a former monastery with *azulejo*-covered walls, serves extremely popular Portuguese dishes and seafood specialities at good prices; light bar snacks also available.

Pap 'Açorda €€–€€€ *Rua da Atalaia 57–9, tel: 213-464 811,* https://papacorda.com. Open Sun, Tue, Wed noon–midnight, Thu–Sat noon–2am. Under glittering chandeliers and against exposed brick walls, this is a cool but disarmingly informal restaurant, popular with a wide-ranging clientele. Traditional and creative Portuguese dishes, with fabulous and filling *açorda real* (a thick shellfish stew with lobster and shrimp) as the main speciality.

Principe do Calhariz €€ *Calçada do Combro 28–30, tel: 213-420 971.* Open Sun–Fri for lunch and dinner. This lively restaurant just beyond the Bica funicular, is a good place to discover local dishes, particularly from northern Portugal where the owners come from. Try *coelho à caçador* (rabbit, hunter's style) or Mirandesa veal steak.

See me Peixaria Mdoerna €€€ *Rua do Loreto 21, tel: 213-461 564,* www.peixariamoderna.com. Open daily for lunch and dinner. This elegant and popular restaurant with simple décor and wooden tables offers a modern take on traditional seafood dishes inspired by Asian flavours. There is also a sushi bar. It has another branch at Time Out Market (Mercado da Ribeira).

Tavares €€€€ *Rua da Misericórdia 37, tel: 213-421 112,* www.restaurante tavares.net. Open Mon–Sat for dinner. A stylish and immensely popular restaurant-café with ornate ceilings, mirrors and chandeliers. Classic French cuisine has been served here for more than a century.

Central Lisbon

Belcanto €€€€ *Largo de São Carlos 10, tel: 213-420 607,* www.belcanto.pt. Open Tue–Sat for lunch and dinner. This stylish, Michelin star restaurant is situated next to São Carlos National Theatre in Chiado. José Avillez, a renowned Portuguese chef, offers a modern interpretation of traditional Portuguese cuisine using the best quality organic ingredients. The tasting menus are outstanding.

Bica do Sapato €€€ *Avenida Infante D. Henrique (Cais da Pedra), tel: 218-810 320,* www.bicadosapato.com. Open Tue–Sat for lunch and dinner, Mon dinner only, Sun 12.30–4pm. This is a trendy restaurant in an old warehouse on the waterfront, across from Santa Apolónia station. Excellent and fairly priced creative Portuguese menu is accompanied by a good list of local wines, and there's a sushi bar on the first floor (dinner only). Closed Jul–Aug.

Cafe Buenos Aires €€ *Calcada Escadinhas do Duque 31 B, tel: 213-420 739,* www.cafebuenosaires.pt. Open daily for dinner. This shabby-chic Argentinian restaurant is a romantic, candlelit, atmospheric place to tuck into superlative steaks and delicious salads. It's perched beside a staircase leading steeply up from the Rossio towards Bairro Alto. Cash only. It has a branch on the nearby Rua do Duque.

Estórias na Casa da Comida €€€€ *Travessa das Amoreiras 1, tel: 213-860 889,* www.casadacomida.pt. Open Mon–Sat for dinner. An elegant restaurant in an old mansion, decorated in soft colours, in northwest Lisbon near the aqueduct. Fine Portuguese cuisine with a modern twist is served outdoors in a patio setting.

Gambrinus €€€€ *Rua das Portas de Santo Antão 23, tel: 213-421 466,* www.gambrinuslisboa.com. Open daily for lunch and dinner (until late). A sophisticated restaurant, one of the city's finest and most famous, in a street of restaurants, close to Rossio. Specialises in traditional Portuguese and Galician dishes.

Leão d'Ouro €€€ *Rua de Dezembro 105, tel: 213-426 195,* www.restau ranteleaodouro.com.pt. Open daily for lunch and dinner. Big, bright, and centrally situated, this *azulejo*-lined restaurant, dating from 1640, is just off the Rossio. Seafood is the speciality. Try the *cataplana* fish stew or the seafood rice with shrimp, lobster, mussels and prawns.

Martinho da Arcada €€€ *Arcadas do Terreiro do Paço/Praça do Comércio 3, tel: 218-879 259*, www.martinhodaarcada.pt. Open Mon–Sat for lunch and dinner. Lisbon's oldest café, under the arcades at Praça do Comércio, dates back to 1782 and has a history littered with political and literary figures – it was a favourite of poet Fernando Pessoa.

Tágide €€€€ *Largo da Academia Nacional de Belas Artes 18, tel: 213-404 010*, www.restaurantetagide.com. Open Mon–Sat for lunch and dinner. Classic Portuguese and French restaurant west of the Praça do Comércio in an elegant, old house offering magnificent views of the waterfront, cathedral and square. There are Port wine tasting sessions and the tapas bar below offers cheaper lunch menu options.

A Travessa €€€ *Travessa do Convento das Bernardas 12, tel: 213-902 034*, http://atravessa.com. Open Mon–Sat for dinner only. A Belgian- and French-influenced menu with dishes such as mussels, stuffed aubergine and bacon-wrapped dates enlivens this good-looking place near Parliament. Mussel feasts on Saturday nights.

York House Restaurant €€€€ *Rua das Janelas Verdes 32, tel: 213-962 435*, www.yorkhouselisboa.com. Open daily for breakfast, lunch (except for Mon–Tue) and dinner. Inhabiting a former 17th-century convent, now the refined and retreat-like York House Hotel, this is a cut above a typical hotel restaurant, with a refined atmosphere and a daily-changing menu featuring imaginative interpretations of Portuguese cuisine. There's a beautiful courtyard. Excellent desserts.

Bélem

O Caseiro €€ *Rua de Belém 35, tel: 213-638 803*. Open Mon–Sat for lunch and dinner. Closed August. In a convenient location between the Coach Museum and the monastery, this is an intimate restaurant serving simple but tasty local dishes. Specialities include *porco á alentejana* (pork, Alentejo style).

A Commenda €€€ *Praça do Império, Belém (inside the Belém Cultural Centre), tel: 213-648 561*, www.ccb.pt. Mon–Sat lunch and dinner, Sun lunch only. Fine river views top the sophisticated atmosphere of this excellent restaurant. Good traditional fish buffet with cod specialities.

Pastéis de Belém € *Rua de Belém 84–92, tel: 213-637 423*, www.pasteisdebelem.pt. Open daily. This legendary purveyor of custard tarts cooks up Lisbon's finest *pastéis de nata*, and its warren-like, tiled interior seats huge numbers of people, all wondering at the deliciousness of these still-warm, delicate pieces of heaven, made to a secret recipe.

São Jerónimo €€ *Rua dos Jerónimos 12, tel: 213-648 796*. Open Mon–Fri for lunch and dinner, Sat for dinner only. A sleek, beautifully designed restaurant with warm woods, dimmed lighting and leather chairs, just around the corner from the Jerónimos Monastery. The menu features creative Portuguese cuisine.

Solar dos Nubes €€€ *Rua dos Luciadas 70, tel: 213-647 359*, www.solardosnunes.com. Open Mon–Sat for lunch and dinner. This stylish restaurant has been awarded a Michelin Bib Gourmand. Offers traditional Portuguese fare and great wine list.

The Docks

Price ranges are the average for restaurants in the Docks.

Doca do Bom Sucesso €€€–€€€€ *Belém*. This small marina in Belém has become a popular nightlife spot for business people and politicos. Restaurants are predictably upmarket and fashionable, including Vela Latina (www.velalatina.pt) and A Margem (www.amargem.com).

Doca Jardim do Tabaco €€–€€€ *Avenida Infante D. Henrique, tel: 218-824 280*. Just in front of Santa Apolónia railway station is a series of popular docks converted into restaurants. They look out over the Tagus as well as the Alfama district. Restaurants in this part include Casanova (http://pizzeriacasanova.pt) and Trigo Latino (www.trigolatino.pt) offering American steaks.

Doca de Santo Amaro €€–€€€€ *Alcântara Mar*. On the Rio Tejo near the 25 de Abril Bridge, Doca de Santo Amaro is the best-known dock and has a lively bar-and-restaurant scene. Most places open daily for lunch and dinner. The best idea is to stroll along the dock and choose a restaurant that looks appealing. Some to keep an eye out for include: 5 Oceanos (www.5oceanos.pt); Doca Peixe (www.docapeixe.com) famous for seafood.

OUTSIDE LISBON

Cozinha Velha €€€ *Palácio Nacional de Queluz, Largo do Palácio, Queluz, tel: 214-356 158*, www.pousadas.pt. Open daily for lunch and dinner. One of the most atmospheric restaurants in Portugal, this was once the old kitchen of the royal palace, but has now been converted into a dining room. It has a garden patio and a decor that will transport you to the 17th century. The regional cooking is excellent. Specialities include stewed partridge with chestnuts and grapes and goat's cheese with walnut and honey wrapped in pastry.

Lawrence Hotel €€€€ *Rua Consigliéri Pedrosa 38–40, Sintra; tel: 219-105 500*, http://lawrenceshotel.com. Open daily for lunch and dinner. The Dutch owners call this 'a restaurant with rooms' rather than a hotel, and Portugal's prime minister is among many who declare it their favourite place to eat. Opened in 1764, it's the oldest hotel in Portugal (Byron stayed here in 1809), and its restaurant is renowned.

A-Z TRAVEL TIPS

A SUMMARY OF PRACTICAL INFORMATION

A Accommodation 113
Airport 113
B Budgeting for
your trip 114
C Camping 115
Car hire 115
Children 116
Climate 116
Clothing 117
Crime and safety 117
Customs
regulations 118
D Disabled travellers 118
Driving 118
E Electricity 120
Embassies and
consulates 121
Emergencies 121
Etiquette 121
G Getting there 121
Guides and tours 123
H Health and
medical care 123

L Language 124
LGBTQ travellers 125
M Maps 126
Media 126
Money 127
O Opening hours 127
P Police 128
Post offices 128
Public holidays 129
R Religion 129
T Telephones 130
Time zones 130
Tipping 131
Toilets 131
Tourist information 131
Transport 132
V Visas and entry
requirements 133
W Websites and
internet access 134
Weights and
measures 134
Y Youth hostels 134

A

ACCOMMODATION (see also Camping, Youth hostels and Recommended hotels on page 135)

Except for family-run *hotéis rurais*, hotels in Portugal are graded from 2-star to 5-star deluxe. The rates are lower in a less elaborate hostelry: an *estalagem* or inn; a *pensão* (rooms with meals available); or *residencial* (rooms, generally without meals). Confusingly, even some elite, intimate inns are often referred to as a *pensão*.

Pousadas are a chain of establishments usually in historic buildings and scenic sites. Ask at tourist offices (see page 131) for a detailed list, or visit the website www.pousadas.pt.

High season runs from mid-June to September, and you should book well ahead, but if a low-season visit is an option, prices are much lower then, and discounts are usually available for longer stays.

When you arrive at your accommodation, you'll usually be asked for your passport and to sign a form which sets out the conditions, prices and room number.

A double/single room **um quarto duplo/simples**

AIRPORT (see also Getting there)

The Aeroporto de Lisboa (www.ana.pt) is only 7km (4 miles) from the city centre, a 15-minute drive (allow twice as long at rush hour). There is a helpful tourist information office at the airport.

The Metro runs from the airport, which is the terminus of the red line from Sãn Sebastião. It takes around 21 minutes to the city centre. Bus No. 91, the AeroBus airport shuttle, leaves about every 20 minutes, 7.40am–10.30pm (from Cais do Sodré) and 7am–11pm (from the airport). It passes through the city centre, stopping at Rossio on the way to Cais do Sodré train station. The ticket (€3.50) can be used all day on trams and buses (though not the Metro). Several local buses (Nos. 745, 705, 208, 83, 44 and 22) also call at the airport (€1.40, 1.80 onboard fare). The AeroShuttle, bus No. 96, serves Gare do Oriente (€3.50), every half hour, 7am–11pm. Taxis are plentiful, and charge about €10–15 to the centre of Lisbon.

> Where do I get the bus to the airport/to the centre of Lisbon? **Onde posso apanhar o autocarro para o aeroporto/para o centro da cidade?**

B

BUDGETING FOR YOUR TRIP

Accommodation. At top levels, hotels in Lisbon compare to those in other large European cities. Still, there are some good prices to be found. A 2-star hotel should be €60–100 for a double; a 3-star €100–150; and for a 4-star, expect to pay over €200. In three categories – historic, design and monuments – *pousadas* are usually priced like 4-star hotels, though the most in-demand historic ones may go higher. Prices usually drop in winter (1 November–1 April). Most prices do not include breakfast but do include 6 percent IVA tax (VAT).

Entertainment. Nightclubs covers are high (€10–20), as are drinks once inside (€7.50 and up). Concert tickets generally range from €10–45.

Flights. Around £100–200 from London.

Local transport. Public transport within the city – buses, trams and the Metro – is not that expensive, with single Metro fares at €1.40, and taxis are affordable and a good way to get around. Most taxi rides within Lisbon's major neighbourhoods will cost no more than €6. Trains to the Estoril Coast are inexpensive (Sintra, €4.30 return).

Meals. Even top-rated restaurants may be affordable compared to most European capitals. Portugal offers a midday meal bargain, the *menu* or *ementa turística*, often no more than €10–15 for a fixed-price, three-course meal. Portuguese wines are good and attractively priced (€10–20), even in fine restaurants. The house wine *(vinho da casa)* is normally good. A three-course dinner in a moderately priced restaurant (for one, with wine) should cost between €25–€35. For an expensive meal in one of Lisbon's prestigious restaurants, expect to pay €50 and up per person.

Museums. Admission fees range about €2.50–5; some days are free. Other sites and attractions may cost between €5 and €10. A Lisboa Card (see page 12) gives discounts.

Sports. Golfing can be expensive, though the courses are excellent: green fees go up to €125. Horse riding costs up to €50 a session.

C

CAMPING

There are several campsites in the Lisbon area, with facilities ranging from basic to elaborate. **Camping Lisboa** (Parque Municipal de Campismo de Monsanto) has 400 individual camping bays and additional bungalows, swimming pool, tennis courts and mini-golf. It's in Monsanto Park, at Estrada de Circunvalação 1500; tel: 217-628 200; www.lisboacamping.com.

Information can be obtained from tourist offices (see page 131) or the Federação Portuguesa de Campismo, Avenida Coronel Eduardo Galhardo 24D; tel: 218-126 890; www.fcmportugal.com.

CAR HIRE (see also Driving)

Major international firms Avis, Hertz, Budget, National and Europcar have desks at the airport and locations in Lisbon; sometimes they also have small satellite offices in other towns. Hotels may recommend local, inexpensive operators. Many companies offer discounts if you book online in advance.

The minimum age for hiring a car is 21–25 (depends on the company), and anyone hiring one must have held a valid licence for at least one year. Rental companies will accept your home country's national driving licence, and you must show your passport. Third-party insurance should be included in the basic charge, but a collision-damage waiver and personal accident policy may be added.

A sub-compact, four-door car with manual transmission, air conditioning, unlimited mileage and mandatory liability insurance usually costs between €150 and €300 per week. Costs may rise in high season (Easter and summer months). Pick-up and drop-off at different points is acceptable without surcharge, though doing either at the airport will incur a supplement.

Avis: tel: 21 754-78 25; www.avis.com.pt.
Europcar: tel: 21 940-77 90; www.europcar.pt.
Hertz: tel: 21 942-63 85; www.hertz.pt.
Holidays Car: tel: 217-150 610; www.holidayscar.com.
Sixt: tel: 218-407 927; www.sixt.com.

> I'd like to hire a car **Queria alugar um carro**
> today/tomorrow **para hoje/amanhã**
> for one day/a week **por um dia/uma semana**

CHILDREN

Portugal is a seriously child friendly country. Children are made welcome just about everywhere, including hotels, restaurants and bars. Watch the strength of the sun in summer months; always ensure your child is wearing a hat and plenty of sunblock. Children's meals are not always available but most restaurants are happy to provide a smaller portion. On public transport children under five travel free, while 5–11-year-olds pay half fare (on trains only).

CLIMATE

Lisbon has an Atlantic climate influenced by the Mediterranean, which produces hot summers and mild winters. Spring and autumn are the best seasons to be in Lisbon, but in the summer, you can bask in the sunshine at the beaches west and south of the capital. The table below gives average air temperatures per month.

	J	F	M	A	M	J	J	A	S	O	N	D
°C	12	12	14	15	18	21	23	24	22	18	15	13
°F	54	54	57	59	64	69	73	75	72	64	59	55

CLOTHING

Unless you come to Lisbon in an unseasonably cold winter, you'll never really have to dress warmly. Spring and autumn are relatively warm, so you won't need anything heavier than a sweater in the daytime and light jacket at night. Summer days can be quite hot, but pack a wrap or sweater for cooler, windy evenings, and rainwear, just in case. An umbrella may be useful in the winter months.

Lisboetas take care over their attire and tend to dress fashionably and fairly formally, but virtually no establishments require a tie. The Estoril Casino 'recommends' that men wear jackets in the evenings. It is respectful not to flash flesh (cover arms and legs) when visiting churches.

CRIME AND SAFETY (see also Emergencies and Police)

Lisbon traditionally has been one of Europe's more laid-back and safe cities, but you should still take the usual precautions. Carry valuables in inside pockets and keep your handbag or camera bag firmly under your arm. Stay alert for pickpockets on buses, trams and in cafés on Rossio, the Alfama area, markets and other tourist spots.

In most parts of the Baixa and Bairro Alto, it is safe to walk at night. Take care around the occasionally seedy Rossio square and narrow, dark and easy-to-get-lost-in streets of the Alfama district at night; if you are going to a *fado* house in the latter, you can take a taxi and have one called when you leave.

The beaches of the Estoril Coast outside Lisbon are quite safe, but it is not a good idea to take any valuables, cameras or purses to the beach. As a general rule, keep valuables in the hotel safe, and refrain from carrying large sums of money or wearing expensive jewellery. Report any theft to the hotel receptionist, the nearest police station or the local tourist office. Leave nothing of value in parked cars, the easiest target for thieves; always lock cars and never leave cases, bags, cameras, etc. in view.

CUSTOMS REGULATIONS

You can bring currency up to €10,000 into the country without declaration. The duty-free allowance for travellers over 17 years of age from non EU countries is 200 cigarettes and 1 litre of spirits or 4 litres of wine. EU residents can bring in 800 cigarettes, plus 10 litres of spirits, 20 litres of fortified wine, 60 litres of sparkling wine, 90 litres of still wine or 110 litres of beer.

D

DISABLED TRAVELLERS

Lisbon's cobbled streets and steep hills don't make it easy for disabled travellers, but areas such as Belém, Baixa and especially Parque das Nações are easier to get around, as they're flat with broad streets and pavements. Some Metro stations, but not all, are equipped for the visually and hearing impaired. To discover which have facilities for the disabled, visit www.metrolisboa.pt. Carris also offer a bus service, for those with reduced mobility, for which you will need to book ahead. Accessible Portugal (www.accessibleportugal.com) offer holidays for the disabled.

DRIVING (see also Car hire)

It is not as tricky driving in Lisbon as some other European capitals, though traffic can be heavy and parking difficult. However, for most visitors, public transport and private taxis are vastly superior methods of navigating the city. To bring your own car into Portugal, you will need your national driving licence, registration papers and insurance – third-party cover is obligatory – and the Green Card that makes your insurance valid in other countries.

Road conditions. The main roads of Portugal are generally in good repair. In order of importance, they are graded as follows: *Auto-Estrada*: motorways (A1–A2, etc.); *Itinerário Principal*: highways (IP); *Itinerário Complementar*: Principal Route (IC); and *Estrada Nacional*: national roads (EN).

Rules and regulations. The rules of the road are the same as in most western European countries. Drive on the right. At roundabouts the vehicle already on the roundabout has priority unless road markings or lights indicate otherwise. Seat belts are compulsory and a heavy fine can be imposed if you are not wearing one.

Speed limits are 120km/h (75mph) on motorways, 100km on roads restricted to motor vehicles, 90km/h (56mph) on other roads and 50km/h (37mph) in urban areas. Minimum speeds are posted (in blue) for some motorway lanes and the suspension bridge across the Tagus. Most motorways have tolls.

Parking. Unless there's an indication to the contrary, you can park for as long as you wish. Certain areas are metered. In 'Blue Zones', you must buy a ticket from a machine for a designated time period; the ticket should then be displayed on the dashboard of the parked car. Car parks and garages are also available. There is a large car park at Gare do Oriente, if you don't want to bring your vehicle into the centre of the city.

Road signs. Standard international pictograms are used but you may encounter the following signs:

cruzamento crossroads
curva perigosa dangerous bend (curve)
descida ingreme steep hill
desvio diversion (detour)
estacionamento permitido parking allowed
estacionamento proíbido no parking
guiar com cuidado drive with care

paragem bus stop
pare stop
passagem proíbida no entry
pedestres/peões pedestrians
perigo danger
proíbida a entrada no entry
seguir pela direita/esquerda keep right/left
sem saída no through road
sentido proíbido no entry
sentido único one-way street
trabalhos roadworks (men at work)
velocidade máxima maximum speed

If you need help. If you belong to a motoring organisation that is affiliated to the Automóvel Clube de Portugal (Rua Rosa Araújo 24, tel: 213-180 100, 707-509 510, www.acp.pt), you can use their emergency and repair services free of charge.

Are we on the right road for...? **É esta a estrada para...?**
Check the oil/tyres/battery, please **Verifique o óleo/os pneus/a bateria, se faz favor.**
I've broken down. **O meu carro está avariado.**
There's been an accident. **Houve um acidente.**

E

ELECTRICITY
Standard throughout Portugal is 220v, 50-cycle AC. For US appliances, 220v transformers and plug adaptors are needed.

EMBASSIES AND CONSULATES

Most embassies and consulates are open Mon–Fri from 9 or 10am until 5pm, with a break in the middle of the day of 1–2 hours.

Australia: Avenida da Liberdade 200, 2°, tel: 213-101 500.
Canada: Avenida da Liberdade 198-200, 3°, tel: 213-164 600.
Ireland: Rua Imprensa 1, 4°, tel: 213-929 440.
South Africa: Avenida Luís Bivar 10, tel: 213-192 200.
UK: Rua de São Bernardo 33, tel: 213-924 000.
US: Avenida das Forças Armadas 16, tel: 217-273 300.

EMERGENCIES (see also Police)

The following numbers are useful 24 hours a day in an emergency:
General emergency **112**
Police **217-654 242**
Ambulance (Red Cross) **219-421 111**
Emergency road service **707-509 510**
Brisa (highways) **808-508 508**

ETIQUETTE

The Portuguese are usually courteous and hospitable. Taking a short while to learn and use the language basics will serve you well. If you are invited to someone's house, it is polite to bring flowers for the hostess. There are always orderly queues at bus stops. Be certain to respect them. Stretching in public is considered rude. Otherwise, use common sense and a smile and you shouldn't go far wrong.

G

GETTING THERE (see also Airport)

By air. Lisbon's airport is linked by regularly scheduled daily non-stop flights from several European cities and from the East Coast of the United States. Flights from Canada, Australia and New Zealand go through London or another European capital. TAP/Air Portugal (www.tap.pt) is Portugal's national airline, and it has wide international links: tel: 707-205 700 from anywhere in Portugal; in Lisbon, 218-415 000; in New York, toll free: 800-221 73 70, 973-624 63 63; in the UK, 0845-601 0932. There are regular TAP and British Airways (www.ba.com) scheduled flights from the UK to Lisbon. Budget airlines offering services from the UK to Lisbon include easyJet (from London Gatwick, Luton, Edinburgh, Liverpool and Bristol; www.easyjet.com) and Ryanair (from London Stansted, Manchester and Dublin; www.ryanair.com). From the US to Lisbon, TAP flies direct from New York, Newark and Boston. Continental (www.continental.com) flies direct from Newark. There are flights to the Portuguese capital on TAP and other carriers from all major European cities.

By sea. Lisbon is a major port, and several cruise ships include a port of call in the capital. Ferries from Great Britain go to Santander and Bilbao, Spain, from Plymouth and Portsmouth (Brittany Ferries; www.brittany-ferries.com). Crossings take 24–36 hours. The drive from northern Spain to Lisbon is then likely to take another 12–14 hours.

By rail. Portugal is linked to the European railway network and connections to Lisbon are possible from points throughout Spain, France and the rest of continental Europe. Travel to Portugal is included on the InterRail Global Pass (www.interrailnet.com) for Europeans, and the Eurail Global Pass (www.eurail.com) for non-Europeans.

The Portuguese national railway network is called **Caminhos de Ferro Portugueses** (tel: 707-210 220, 808-208 208; www.cp.pt). The Santa Apolónia station (Avenida Dom Henrique, tel: 211-022 000) serves all international trains.

Daily international trains run between Paris and Lisbon (Sud Express), crossing the frontier at Vilar Formoso; between Lisbon and Madrid, crossing the frontier at Marvão; and between Oporto and Vigo, crossing the frontier at Valença.

By car. Major motorways connect Portugal with Spain at numerous border points. The fastest route from Oporto is the A1 *autoestrada*; from Madrid, take A2, crossing into the city at the Ponte 25 de Abril. The drive from Madrid to Lisbon is 8–10 hours; from Paris, 20–22 hours.

GUIDES AND TOURS

Information on tours currently on offer is available at tourist offices or from your hotel.

Carristur (www.carristur.pt), operated by the city's bus company, has tram and bus tours starting in the Praça do Comércio. Trams travel the Circuito Descobrimentos to Belém and the Eléctrico das Colinas around the city hills; open-top buses go to the Parque das Nações and Belém.

Cityrama-Grayline (www.cityrama.pt) open-top bus tours start from Praça Marquês de Pombal. Carristur (www.carris.pt) also operates a four-hour sightseeing tour of Sintra.

All of the major excursion firms offer trips to Cascais, Estoril, Mafra, Queluz and Sintra, as well as a long day's outing covering major sites north of Lisbon: Fátima, Alcobaça and Batalha, Óbidos and Nazaré. If you are travelling independently, you can cover all these at greater leisure, even making an overnight stop or two on the way.

Transtejo runs regular ferries across the River Tagus, including from Cais do Sodré to Cacilhas and between Belém and Porto Brandhão (tel: 808-203 050, www.transtejo.pt).

H

HEALTH AND MEDICAL CARE

Standards of hygiene in Lisbon, and in Portugal as a whole, are generally very high; the most likely illness to befall travellers will be due to an excess of sun or alcohol. The water is safe to drink, but bottled water is available everywhere. Ask for *água com gas* (carbonated) or *sem gas* (still).

Farmácias (chemists/drugstores) are open during normal business hours, and one shop in each neighbourhood is on duty round the clock. Addresses are listed in newspapers and on pharmacy doors. To locate night pharmacies, tel: 118.

For more serious illness or injuries, there is also a **British Hospital** (XXI, Rua Tomás da Fonseca Edifícios B e F, Torres de Lisboa, tel: 217-213 400), which has English-speaking staff. Check your medical insurance to be sure it covers illness or accident while you are abroad. EU nationals with a European Health Insurance Card (EHIC), obtained before departure (from post offices or online at www.ehic.org.uk in the UK), can receive free emergency treatment at Social Security and Municipal hospitals in Portugal. Privately billed hospital visits are expensive.

I need a doctor/dentist **Preciso de um médico/ dentista**
Get a doctor quickly. **Chame um médico, depressa.**
Where's the nearest pharmacy? **Aonde é a farmácia (de guardia) mais perto?**
an ambulance **uma ambulância**
hospital **hospital**
upset stomach **mal de estômago**
sunstroke **uma insolação**
fever **febre**

L

LANGUAGE

Portuguese, a derivative of Latin, is spoken in Brazil, Angola, Mozambique and Macau – all former colonies of Portugal. Any high-school Spanish may help with signs and menus, but will not unlock the mysteries of spoken Portuguese. The Portuguese spoken in Portugal is much more closed and gutteral-sounding, and is also spoken much faster than in Brazil.

Almost everyone in Portugal understands Spanish, many speak French and a surprising number of people in Lisbon can speak passable English. Schoolchildren are taught French and English.

The *Berlitz Portuguese Phrasebook* covers most situations you're likely to encounter during a visit to Portugal. Also useful is the *Berlitz Portuguese–English/English–Portuguese Pocket Dictionary*, containing a menu-reader supplement (www.berlitzpublishing.com).

Do you speak English? **Fala inglês?**
excuse me/you're welcome **perdão/de nada**
please **faz favor**
thank you **obrigado/a**
where/when/how **onde/quando/como**
day/week/month/year **dia/semana/mês/ano**
left/right **esquerda/direita**
near/far **perto/longe**
cheap/expensive **barato/caro**
open/closed **aberto/fechado**
hot/cold **quente/frio**
old/new **velho/novo**
Please write it down. **Escreva-lo, por favor.**
What does this mean? **Que quer dizer isto?**
Help me, please. **Ajude-me, por favor.**
Just a minute. **Um momento.**
What time is it? **Que horas são?**
Sunday **domingo**
Monday **segunda-feira**
Tuesday **terça-feira**
Wednesday **quarta-feira**
Thursday **quinta-feira**
Friday **sexta-feira**
Saturday **sábado**
What day is it today? **Que dia é hoje?**
yesterday **ontem**
today **hoje**
tomorrow **amanhã**

LGBTQ TRAVELLERS

In a country heavily influenced by the Roman Catholic Church, attitudes towards gays and lesbians are not as tolerant in Portugal as some other places in Europe.

Lisbon is the most important city in Portugal's gay scene, and offers a number of bars and clubs catering for a gay crowd, including Bar 106 (Rua de São Marcal 106); the scene centres around Praça do Príncipe Real, close to Bairro Alto. Also, on the Costa da Caparica, the west coast of the peninsula across the Tagus, beach No. 9 on the narrow-gauge railway is also a popular hangout.

As yet, there are no helplines. A good website with information on travel, bars and beaches is www.portugalgay.pt.

M

MAPS

Tourist information offices have free maps of Lisbon and the surrounding area, as well as a Carris map of the tram, bus and elevator network. Towns on the tourist circuit, such as Óbidos, Sintra, Cascais and Estoril, also make free maps available through their tourist information offices.

MEDIA

Europe's principal newspapers, including most British dailies, and the *International Herald Tribune*, are available on the day of publication at many newsagents and hotels. Popular foreign magazines are also sold at the same shops or stands. The most important Portuguese-language daily are Correio da Manhã and *Diário de Notícias*, which contains cultural listings.

Free listings publications, such as *Follow Me Lisboa, Agenda Cultural Lisboa* and *Tips*, are widely available. *Portugal News*, an English-language weekly published in the Algarve, covers stories from around the country (www.theportugalnews.com).

Four television channels are widely available in Portugal: two are government-run and two are independent. Foreign films, whether made-for-TV or original cinematic productions, are usually shown in the original language with subtitles. Most hotels have access to satellite TV. The government operates four radio channels.

MONEY

Currency *(moeda)*. The euro (€) is the official currency used in Portugal. Notes are denominated in 5, 10, 20, 50, 100, 200 and 500 euros; coins in 1 and 2 euros and 1, 2, 5, 10, 20 and 50 cents *(centimos)*.

Currency exchange *(banco, câmbio)*. Normal banking hours are Mon–Fri 8.30am–3pm. There is a 24-hour exchange office at the airport.

Credit cards *(cartão de crédito)*. International credit cards are widely accepted. However, in some shops and restaurants, especially in small towns outside Lisbon, you may not be able to use a credit card. Police fines cannot be paid by credit card.

Tax refunds. For non-EU residents, the IVA tax (VAT) imposed on most goods can be refunded on purchases of at least €49.88 in a single store. Look for the blue-and-white tax-free sign in stores. To obtain the rebate, fill in a form provided by the shop where you purchase the goods. One copy is kept by the shop; the others must be presented at customs upon departure. The refund can be credited to your credit card at the airport or posted to your home address after your return.

Can I pay with this credit card? **Posso pagar com cartão de crédito?**
I want to change some pounds/dollars. **Queria trocar libras/ dólares.**
Can you cash a travellers' cheque? **Pode pagar um cheque de viagem?**

O

OPENING HOURS

Banks open 8.30am–3pm. The majority of shops and offices open 9 or

10am–7pm weekdays, and Sat 9am–1pm. Most museums are closed on Mon and public holidays (the tourist office has a list of those open on Mon); palaces are closed on either Mon or Tue. On every other day (including Sun) they are open 10 or 11am–5pm, but many close noon–2pm or 1–2.30pm. Many shopping centres around Lisbon and the suburbs have extended opening hours, closing at 10pm or midnight, including Sun.

P

POLICE (see also Crime and safety and Emergencies)

The Portuguese national police, identified by their blue uniforms, are generally helpful and friendly, and often speak a little English. Policemen assigned to traffic duty wear red armbands with a silver letter 'T' (for *trânsito*, or traffic) on a red background, a white helmet and white gloves.

On highways, traffic is controlled by the Guarda Nacional Republicana (GNR) in white-and-red or white-and-blue cars, or on motorcycles. Occasionally they make spot-checks on documents or tyres, and can issue on-the-spot fines, payable in cash only.

Lisbon's police headquarters are in Largo Penha de França 1, 2nd floor, tel: 218-111 000. Call the tourist police on tel: 213-421 623. The emergency number is **112**.

> Where's the nearest police station? **Onde fica o posto de polícia mais próximo?**

POST OFFICES

The mail service is efficient, with British-style red pillar boxes. Local post offices are open Mon–Fri 9am–6pm. Major branch offices also operate on Sat until noon. A 24-hour office can be found at the airport. Lisbon's main post office is in Praça dos Restauradores (opposite the tourist office). You can purchase stamps from some tobacconists and kiosks, as well as at post offices.

> A stamp for this letter/postcard, please. **Um selo para esta carta/este postal, por favor.**

PUBLIC HOLIDAYS

1 January *Ano Novo* New Year's Day
25 April *Dia da Liberdade* 1974 Revolution Day
1 May *Dia do Trabalhador* May Day
10 June *Dia de Camões* Camões's Day
15 August *Assunção* The Assumption
5 October *Implantaçao da República* Republic Day
1 November *Todos-os-Santos* All Saints' Day
1 December *Dia da Independencia* Independence Day
8 December *Imaculada Conceição* Immaculate Conception
25 December *Natal* Christmas Day
Moveable dates
Carnaval (Shrove Tuesday/Carnival), *Sexta-feira Santa* (Good Friday) and *Corpo de Deus* (Corpus Christi).
Local holidays
Lisbon, Estoril and Cascais have a local holiday on 13 June in honour of St Anthony (Santo António). Sintra has a holiday on 29 June (São Pedro).

R

RELIGION

The Portuguese are predominantly Roman Catholic, a fact reflected in surviving religious rituals and saints' days that are public holidays. The shrine at Fátima is one of the most important pilgrimages in Catholicism. The tourist information office has a list of services for English-speaking Catholics as well as other services. Dress modestly when visiting religious sites.

T

TELEPHONES

Portugal's country code is **351**. The local area code – **21** in the case of Lisbon and the Estoril Coast, including Sintra – must be dialled before all phone numbers, including local calls (nine digits in total).

Most Portugal public telephones *(PT Comunicações)* accept pre-paid telephone cards, which are available throughout the city. Telephone cards can be purchased at kiosks and newsagents in various denominations. Most phone boxes also accept credit cards, an inexpensive and easy way of making any call. Local, national and international calls made from hotels almost always carry an exorbitant surcharge. Use an international calling card if you must call from your hotel room.

The cheapest way to call is usually via Skype or other similar services. Portugal is on the GSM 900/1800 network, compatible with Europe, Australia and much of Asia.

Dialling internationally is straightforward: dial 00 for an international line (both Europe and overseas) plus the country code (UK 44, US 1) plus the phone number (including the area code, without the initial '0' where there is one).

TIME ZONES

Portugal, being at the western edge of Europe, maintains Greenwich Mean Time (GMT), along with the UK, and is therefore one hour behind the rest of the EU. From the last Sunday in March until the last Sun in October, the clocks are moved one hour ahead for summer time, GMT + 1.

In summer the chart looks like this:

New York	London	**Lisbon**	Paris	Sydney	Auckland
7am	noon	**noon**	1pm	9pm	11pm

TIPPING

Hotel and restaurant bills are generally all-inclusive, but an additional tip of 5–10 percent is common.

Hotel porters generally receive around €0.50–€1 for each bag that they carry, while hairdressers and taxi drivers are normally tipped about 10 percent and tour guides 10–15 percent. Toilet attendants should be tipped about €0.25 and your hotel room cleaner should be given around an extra €0.50 per day.

TOILETS

Public toilets can be found in many public places, including stations, museums and large stores. Toilets are marked *Senhoras* (ladies) and *Homens* (men).

> Where are the toilets? **Onde é o lavabo/quarto de banho?**

TOURIST INFORMATION

Portuguese National Tourist Offices (ICEP, or Investimentos, Comércio e Turismo de Portugal; www.turismodeportugal.pt) are maintained in many countries, including the following:

Ireland: 25/26 Windsor Place, Lower Pembroke Street, Dublin 2, tel: 353 353-01-412 7050

UK: Portuguese National Tourist Office, 11 Belgrave Square, London SW1X 8PP, tel: 020-7201 6666, 0845-355 1212, www.visitportugal.com.

US: Portuguese National Tourist Office, 590 Fifth Avenue, New York, NY 10036, tel: 1 646-723 02 00.

The main tourist information office for the city is the **Lisboa Welcome Centre**, Rua do Arsenal 15, in Praça do Comércio, tel: 210-312 700. There is also a tourist office for the city as well as for the country in the **Palácio Foz**, on the west side of Praça dos Restauradores, tel: 213-463 314; also at the **Airport Arrivals Terminal** (tel: 218-450 660) and at

Santa Apolónia station (tel: 218-821 606). A useful tourist information **helpline** is available on tel: 800-209 209.

Where is the tourist office? **Onde é o turismo?**

TRANSPORT

Buses: Local. You can get a free map of the entire transit system at tourist information offices, or at information posts of **Carris** (www.carris.pt), the transport authority, which are dotted all over the city. They also sell economical 1-day passes *(bilhete/passe turístico)*, which can be used on buses, trams and the Metro, tel: 213-613 000. Pay the driver or show him your prepaid ticket before validating it in the clipping machine.

Buses: Inter-city. Lisbon's bus terminals serve different parts of the country. Ask for information about bus routes at the tourist office in Praça dos Restauradores.

Trams. Tram stops are indicated by large signs marked *paragem* (stop). The Carris bus map shows tram routes as well. The most popular tourist tram is the No. 28, which goes from Bairro Alto to Alfama and the castle. Most trams are entered at the front, where you buy a ticket from the driver. On funiculars you pay at the door.

Metro. Lisbon's underground Metropolitano (www.metrolisboa.pt) has four colour-coded lines. The red line runs all the way to the airport. Certain stations link up with railway stations and ferry termini. The cheapest way to travel is to buy an electronic Viva Viagem card (€0.50), available at station vending machines and ticket offices, which you then charge up as you go. You can also charge it for a 24-hour session, which costs €5, and is valid for unlimited journeys on the Metro and Carris networks (the latter includes funiculars such as the Elevador de Santa Justa). Children under four travel free on the Metro.

Trains. Lisbon has four railway stations. The main ones for national and international travel are Santa Apolónia (reached by bus No. 9 or 9A from

Avenida da Liberdade) and Estação do Oriente (Oriente Metro). Commuter trains for the western suburbs, Estoril and Cascais depart from Cais do Sodré, on the waterfront, while trains for Sintra and the west depart from Rossio station.

Taxis. Lisbon's metered taxis, often Mercedes, are beige, and indicated by a sign reading TAXI. The fare is shown on the meter – check that it's running. Drivers add 20 percent from 9pm to 6am and extra if you have over 30kg (66lb) of baggage. To request a taxi, tel: 218-119 000, 217-932 756 or 218-111 100. In rural areas, cars marked 'A' (meaning *aluguer*, 'for hire') operate as taxis without meters.

Ferries. The two main ferry stations for the River Tagus's southern shore are Estação Fluvial Terreiro do Paço for Barreiro, and Cais do Sodré for Cacilhas, Montijo and Seixal.

> How much is a ticket to...? **Quanto é o bilhete para ...?**
> Will you tell me when to get off? **Pode dizer-me quando devo descer?**
> Where's the nearest bus/tram stop? **Onde fica a mais próxima paragem dos autocarros/eléctricos?**
> Where can I get a taxi? **Onde posso encontrar um táxi?**
> What's the fare to...? **Quanto custa o percurso até ...?**

V

VISAS AND ENTRY REQUIREMENTS

You need a valid passport for a visit to Portugal. EU tourists may stay for up to 90 days; for longer stays they need to apply for a permit. US, Canadian, Australian and New Zealand tourists may also stay for up to 90 days without a visa. All other foreign nationals must apply for a visa.

Customs. If you are a non-EU resident, you may be able to reclaim VAT on some items bought within Portugal – look out for shops with the sign 'Tax

Free Shopping' in the window. The minimum spend in one store on the same day is €61,35. You will need to complete a form and present it when you are leaving the country, along with the purchased goods.

W

WEBSITES AND INTERNET ACCESS

The most useful websites are:
www.visitlisboa.com The Welcome Centre city tourist office
www.visitportugal.com The official Portuguese tourism site
www.portugal.com Travel and tourism site
www.portugalvirtual.pt General information and accommodation
www.tap.pt TAP/Air Portugal, the national airline
www.cp.pt Caminhos de Ferro Portugueses, the railway network
www.pousadas.pt For the government-owned *pousadas*

The Welcome Centre in Praça do Comércio has Internet facilities and can give information on other *(ciber)* cafés all over the city.

WEIGHTS AND MEASURES

Portugal uses the metric system of weights and measures.

Y

YOUTH HOSTELS

It is best to join Hostelling International before you depart (www.hihostels.com), but you can join up on arrival. The headquarters of the Portuguese Youth Hostel Association are at Rua Lúcio de Azevedo 27, Lisbon; reservations tel: 707-203 030; www.pousadasjuventude.pt.

They run hostels in central Lisbon at Rua Andrade Corvo 46, tel: 213-532 696, dorm beds cost €12.50–18 and doubles €36–46; in the Parque das Nações at Rua de Moscavide Lt 47–101, tel: 218-920 890, dorm beds cost €8–16 and doubles €34–40; and in Almada at Quinta do Bucelinho, tel: 212-943 491, dorm beds cost €8–16 and doubles €34–42.

RECOMMENDED HOTELS

Hotel prices have risen in recent years to match most Western European destinations, and at the top level they are surpassing popular cities like Barcelona. Many hotels offer special packages, such as summer or weekend reductions. Central Lisbon covers the area from the waterfront, Bairro Alto, Lapa and Avenida da Liberdade. North Lisbon refers to the area around and beyond Praça Marquês de Pombal. *Pousadas*, found beyond Lisbon, are well-managed chain hotels; the ones listed occupy historic buildings, and their restaurants are usually among the town's best.

The price indication is for a double room, with breakfast, including service and taxes in high season (April–October). In low season prices can be considerably less, and top hotels also often offer discounts for booking early at any time of year. All the hotels take major credit cards unless otherwise stated.

€€€€€	over 200 euros
€€€€	150–200 euros
€€€	100–150 euros
€€	60–100 euros
€	below 60 euros

LISBON

Albergaria Senhora do Monte €€€ *Calçada do Monte 39, tel: 218-866 002*. Perched on a hillside in Graça, a district northeast of Baixa, this simple-looking place offers good accommodation with views of the castle and the river. It has a garden courtyard, where guests can have breakfast, and a top floor bar.

As Janelas Verdes €€€€€ *Rua das Janelas Verdes 47, tel: 213-968 143, booking: 213 218 200*; www.asjanelasverdes.com. An elegant hotel in the sophisticated Lapa district, near the River Tagus and the Museu de Arte Antiga. This small hotel occupies the 18th-century townhouse of one of Portugal's most famous writers, Eça de Queirós, and the house next door. It has a quiet, garden-like courtyard and top-floor library. Some rooms have superb views of the river. Wheelchair access.

Hotel Avenida Palace €€€€ *Rua 1 de Dezembro 123, tel: 213-218 100*, www.hotelavenidapalace.pt. Situated right on Rossio, the major plaza in the Baixa district, the remodelled Avenida Palace is one of Lisbon's finest luxury hotels. Built in 1892, it has a magnificent, old-fashioned elegance, with sumptuous public rooms and beautiful, classically decorated accommodation. Sybarites can opt for the Louis XVI-style room. The gym offers modern fitness facilities. Wheelchair access. Regular jazz and classical music concerts.

Bairro Alto Hotel €€€€€ *Praça Luís de Camões 2, tel: 213-408 288*, www.bairroaltohotel.com. Ultra-chic, this boutique hotel in the bohemian Bairro Alto district, in the historic heart of Lisbon, is a short walk from the main sights. Rooms are soundproofed against city noise, and have plasma TVs and upmarket styling. The terrace and café bar are relaxing places to hang out for a drink.

Hotel Borges €€ *Rua Garrett 108, tel: 210-456 400*, www.hotelborges.com. A typical old Lisbon hotel with a lot of character, the Borges has an excellent location right in the heart of the Chiado district. Spacious rooms, renovated in 2012, include satellite TV and Wi-Fi. Some have balconies.

Hotel Britania €€€€ *Rua Rodrigues Sampaio 17, tel: 213-155 016*, www.heritage.pt. Owned by the same family that runs other top, intimate hotels in Lisbon, the Britania, in a historic 1940s townhouse, may be the most comfortable of them all. The rooms are spacious and elegantly appointed, with marble bathrooms. The hotel, alongside Avenida da Liberdade, has been lovingly restored with genuine Art Deco touches, such as the bar. Wheelchair access.

Hotel do Chiado €€€€ *Rua Nova do Almada 114, tel: 213-256 100*, www.hoteldochiado.com. This chic hotel occupies part of the building housing the Armazéns do Chiado shopping mall, in the heart of the Chiado district. In keeping with the upmarket surroundings, the lobby and rooms are very design-oriented, with traditional Portuguese styling. There are superb views over Alfama from the roof terrace.

Dom Pedro Palace €€€€€ *Avenida Engenheiro Duarte Pacheco 24, tel: 213-896 600,* www.dompedro.com. A swish five-star hotel, with the city's swankiest entrance, this mirrored high-rise is just north of Parque Eduardo VII and across from the Amoreiras shopping centre. Rooms, equipped with every luxury, have spectacular views of the city. Dom Pedro has supplanted more traditional luxury hotels in Lisbon. Popular with American tourists and European business travellers, it has a top-flight Italian restaurant and a bistro-style café. Wheelchair access.

Ever Lisboa City Center Hotel €€–€€€ *Avenida da Liberdade 189, tel: 213-522 618,* www.galahotels.com. A small, historic hotel right on the main boulevard, this former 19th-century Venetian-style palace has a spectacular spiral staircase and period touches, such as stained-glass windows, throughout. The economy rooms can be dark. Wheelchair access.

Hotel Expo Astória €€ *Rua Braancamp 10, tel: 213-861 317.* This mid-size, 1920s-style hotel is a handsome place, with spacious rooms, in an elite part of town. Just off Praça Marquês de Pombal, it ranks as a bargain.

Four Seasons Hotel Ritz Lisboa €€€€€ *Rua Rodrigo da Fonseca 88, tel: 213-811 400,* www.fourseasons.com. One of Lisbon's oldest luxury hotels has an ugly Soviet-style exterior that could not be a greater contrast to its swanky interior, which provides the height of indulgence. Rooms with balconies offer good views over Parque Eduardo VII and busy Pombal square. Excellent restaurant, Veranda. Wheelchair access.

Inspira Santa Marta €€€ *Rua de Santa Marta 48, tel: 210-440 900;* www.inspirahotels.com. Near the Avenida da Liberdade, this relatively new hotel (built in 2010) is a designer place with admirable eco-credentials – it uses green technology, runs according to sustainable policies and supports charitable projects. Rooms are modelled around Feng Shui principles. There are two rooms for guests with disabilities.

Internacional Design Hotel €€€€€ *Rua da Betesga 3, tel: 213-240 990*, www.idesignhotel.com. This emphatically designer hotel, in a great location overlooking Rossio, Lisbon's main square, has four types of highly conceptualised, spectacular rooms – Urban, Tribe, Zen and Pop – with magazine looks and every comfort. Wheelchair access.

Jerónimos 8 €€€ *Rua dos Jerónimos 8, tel: 213-600 900*, www.almeida hotels.pt. Go boutique in Belém at this stylish place, with sleek rooms that combine strong and neutral colours to harmonious effect. There are great views over the monastery. The Busaco Wine Bar serves rare Portuguese wines and the delicious, traditional *pastéis de Belém* custard tarts.

Lapa Palace €€€€€ *Rua Pau da Bandeira 4, tel: 213-949 494*, www.olissip pohotels.com. This lovingly detailed conversion of an old palatial mansion overlooks the River Tagus in Lapa. Opened in 1992, it remains the trendsetter in Lisbon luxury. It is surrounded by landscaped gardens, and there is an outdoor pool. Rooms are plush, with *azulejo*-decorated bathrooms; the entrance is swathed in marble and ceiling frescos. Wheelchair access.

Lisboa Plaza €€€ *Travessa do Salitre 7 (off Avenida Liberdade), tel: 213-218 200*, www.heritage.pt. This stylish, family-run hotel, on a quiet but convenient street, opened in the 1950s. Rooms are very comfortable, with every detail carefully overseen by a noted Portuguese designer. A restaurant serves Portuguese specialities and a generous buffet breakfast. Wheelchair access.

Pensão Londres € *Rua Dom Pedro V 53, tel: 213-462 203*, www.pensao londres.com.pt. An unpretentious *pensão* at the edge of the Bairro Alto, occupying four floors of an imposing town house just minutes away from the district's restaurants, *fado* houses, bars and clubs. There are panoramic views of the city from rooms on the 3rd and 4th floors; otherwise take in the vista from the nearby Miradouro de São Pedro de Alcântara. The rooms are small but adequately furnished, though not all have private bathrooms or toilets. Continental breakfast included.

Hotel Métropole €€€€ *Praça do Dom Pedro V 30, tel: 213-219 030*. One of Lisbon's best deals, is this classic 1920s Art Deco hotel is in the heart of the Baixa, overlooking Rossio. Rooms are generously sized and outfitted with antiques. Some rooms have castle, Baixa and Alfama views. Wheelchair access.

Pensão Residencial Ninho das Aguias € *Costa do Castelo 74, tel: 218-854 070*. The 'eagle's nest' next to the castle is the most delightfully eccentric *pensão* in town, but it is not for the faint-hearted – you need to negotiate not only Alfama's cobbled streets but also the building's spiral staircase. The rewards are wonderful: a romantic flower-filled terrace with great views. Book well ahead as this place is very popular. Cash only.

Solar dos Mouros €€€–€€€€ *Rua Milagre de Santo António 6, tel: 218-854 940, http://solardosmouroslisboa.com/*. A stylish boutique hotel up near the castle, occupies a tangerine-coloured townhouse and enjoys panoramic views over the Tagus and city. The contemporary rooms are individually designed with bold colours, African art and striking modern paintings; they also feature marble bathrooms and hardwood floors.

Hotel Tivoli Lisboa €€€€€ *Avenida da Liberdade 185, tel: 213-198 900, www.tivolihotels.com*. One of Lisbon's largest and longest-running luxury hotels, the Tivoli is right on the main thoroughfare. It excels in services and facilities, which include the noted rooftop Terraço restaurant and a heated outdoor swimming pool. Outdoor dining in summer. Wheelchair access.

VIP Executive Suites Éden €€€ *Praça dos Restauradores 24, tel: 213-216 600, www.viphotels.com*. In a famous Art Deco building right on Praça dos Restauradores, this cool, modern apartment-hotel is a great deal, especially for families. There are kitchen-equipped studios and full apartments, with daily or weekly maid service. Panoramic pool and breakfast service. Wheelchair access.

York House €€€–€€€€ *Rua das Janelas Verdes 32, tel: 213-962 435, www.yorkhouselisboa.com*. Near the Museu de Arte Antiga in Lapa, several blocks west of the centre, this small, converted 17th-century Carmelite convent overlooks the River Tagus. It retains the feel of a serene retreat from the outside world, and rooms are elegant but not stuffy. There's outdoor dining in the garden courtyard during the summer and a recommended restaurant. Wheelchair access.

ESTORIL COAST

Hotel Albatroz €€€€€ *Rua Frederico Arouca 100, Cascais, tel: 214-847 380*, www.albatrozhotels.com. This mansion perched above the Praia da Rainha beach is Cascais's most elegant hotel. Public rooms and guest rooms swim in luxury, with some occupying another beautiful palace across the street. Outdoor pool and good restaurant with superb views.

Hotel Fortaleza do Guincho €€€€–€€€€€ *Estrada do Guincho, Cascais, tel: 214-870 491*, www.fortalezadoguincho.com. Just outside of Cascais, in a former 16th-century fortress perched on a rocky ledge overlooking Guincho beach and the sea, this enchanting hotel is a remarkable getaway. Marvellous antique touches throughout include tile floors and period silver and crystal. Most rooms have fireplaces, and many have balconies with views of the sea – including Cabo da Roca, Europe's westernmost point.

Hotel Palácio do Estoril €€€€€ *Rua Particular, Estoril, tel: 214-648 000*, www.palacioestorilhotel.com. This 5-star luxury hotel, established in 1930, looks like a cruise ship and is as palatial as its name suggests. It has a heated outdoor pool, tennis courts and gardens, and offers guests special rates at its golf course. Top-notch restaurant, Four Seasons Grill, offers international cuisine. Wheelchair access.

QUELUZ AND SINTRA

Pousada de Queluz, D. Maria I €€€–€€€€ *Largo do Palácio Nacional, Queluz, tel: 214-356 158*, www.pousadas.pt. Occupying the part of the royal summer palace that was formerly the domain of the Royal Guard of the Court, this pink and white *pousada* is ideal if you want to explore Lisbon and its surroundings but don't want to stay in the city. The rooms are attractive and well sized, and restaurant Cozinha

Velha, across the road, which serves the delicious Marfim pudding, is one of the area's best.

Tivoli Palácio de Seteais €€€€–€€€€€ *Rua Barbosa do Bocage 10, Sintra, tel: 219-233 200*, www.minorhotels.com. A luxury hotel in a beautiful 18th-century palace, with antique furniture, manicured gardens (Lord Byron wrote here) and superb views. Some visitors find it a little dainty compared to more relaxed *quintas* nearby. Sports facilities include tennis courts, an outdoor pool and horse riding.

SOUTH OF LISBON

Hotel Club Azeitão €€€ *Quinta Do Bon Pastor, Vila Fresca de Azeitão, tel: 212-198 590*, www.turim-hotels.com. This nice, old-fashion hotel is just 20 minutes from Lisbon. Amenities include a swimming pool, tennis court, business centre, restaurant and coffee shop. The green terrace is a good place to relax. Nearby is a beautiful golf course. In low season the price for a double room drops to €55.

Pousada de Palmela €€€€€ *Castelo de Palmela, Palmela, tel: 212-351 226*, www.pousadas.pt. A luxury *pousada* carved out of a 12th-century hilltop castle, later a headquarters of the Order of Santiago, with a quiet cloister. There are fabulous views towards Setúbal and the sea. The notable restaurant in the former refectory serves local dishes; its specialities are cod and partridge.

Sana Sesimbra Hotel €€€ *Avenida 25 de Abril, Sesimbra, tel: 212-289 000*, www.sesimbra.sanahotels.com. Modern and stylish, this hotel is just across the road from the main beach. Facilities include a restaurant and bar, and a rooftop pool with panoramic views of the bay.

Pousada de Setúbal, São Filipe €€€€€ *Forte de São Filipe, Setúbal, tel: 265-550 070*, www.pousadas.pt. A *pousada* inside the walls of a fortress built in 1590, overlooking the port of Setúbul. There are great views of the Sado estuary and Tróia peninsula. Some rooms are in the former castle dungeons. Close to the Serra de Arrábida National Park.

INDEX

Alfama 28
Aqueduto das Águas Livres 59
Atlântico Hall 62
Avenida da Liberdade 42
Azurara Palace 30
Bairro Alto 39, 42
Baixa 37
Beco da Cardosa 31
Beco do Carneiro 31
Belém 48
Boca do Inferno 76
Cabo da Roca 77
Cabo Espichel 79
Calouste Gulbenkian
Casa Bocage (Setúbal) 81
Casa do Alentejo 40
Casa dos Bicos 35
Cascais 74
Castelo de São Jorge 33
Castelo dos Mouros 69
Cathedrall 35
Cemitério dos Ingleses 46
Centro Cultural de Belém 54
Centro de Arte Moderna 58
Cervejeria da Trindade 44
Chiado 45
Colares 71
Costa do Estoril 73
Cristo Rei, statue of 63
Doca de Santo Amaro 48
Doca do Alcântara 48
Elevador de Glória 43
Elevador de Santa Justa 39
Ericeira 73
Estação do Oriente 60
Estação do Rossio 41
Estoril 73
Estufa Fria 55
Estufa Quente 56

Fragata D. Fernando II e Glória 48
Galeria Municipal do Banco de Portugal (Setúbal) 81
Guincho 77
Igreja de Jesus (Setúbal) 80
Igreja de Santo António da Sé 35
Igreja de Santo Estêvão 31
Igreja de São Miguel 31
Igreja de São Roque 43
Igreja do Carmo 44
Igreja e Mosteiro de São Vicente de Fora 32
Jardim Botânico 43
Jardim da Estrela 46
Lapa 46
Largo Barão Quintela 45
Largo das Portas do Sol 30
Largo de São Rafael 30
Lisboa Welcome Centre 38
Mafra 71
Miradouro de Santa Luzia 29
Miradouro de São Pedro de Alcântara 43
Montserrate Palace Gardens 70
Mosteiro dos Jerónimos 51
MUDE-Museu do Design e da Moda 38
Museu Archeológico do Carmo 44
Museu Colecção Berardo 54
Museu da Marinha 53

Museu de Água 59
Museu de Arte Sacra 44
Museu de Artes Decorativas 30
Museu de Cidade (Setúbal) 80
Museu do Chiado 45
Museu do Fado 28
Museu do Mar – Rei Dom Carlos (Cascais) 76
Museu dos Condes de Castro Guimarães (Cascais) 75
Museu do Teatro Romano 28
Museu Gulbenkian 57
Museu Militar 36
Museum of Art, Architecture and Technology 49
Museum of Modern Art (Sintra) 70
Museu Nacional de Arqueologia 53
Museu Nacional de Arte Antiga 46
Museu Nacional do Azulejo 36
Museu Nacional dos Coches 49
Oceanário de Lisboa 61
Paços do Concelho (Cascais) 75
Padrão dos Descobrimentos 54
Palácio da Ajuda 50
Palácio da Pena 69
Palácio de Seteais (Sintra) 70
Palácio Foz 41
Palácio Nacional de Mafra 71

Palácio Nacional de Queluz 64
Palácio Nacional de Sintra 67
Palácio São Bento 46
Panteão Nacional 32
Parque das Nações 61
Parque Eduardo VII 55
Parque Natural da Arrábida 79
Pavilhão do Conhecimento 61
Planetário 54
Ponte 25 de Abril 63
Ponte Vasco da Gama 60
Portinho da Arrábida 80
Portugal Pavilion 62
Praça da Figueira 41
Praça do Comércio 37
Praça dos Restauradores 41
Praça Marquês de Pombal 42
Praça Martim Moniz 41
Praia das Maçãs 71
Quinta da Regaleira 70
Rossio 39
Rua de São João da
Praça 30
Rua de São Pedro 31
Rua dos Bacalhoeiros 36
Sé Patriarcal 34
Serra da Arrábida 79
Serra de Sintra 77
Sesimbra 77
Setúbal 80
Sintra 66
Teatro Camões 62
Teatro Nacional Dona Maria II 40
Torre de Belém 55
Torre Vasco da Gama 61

INSIGHT GUIDES POCKET GUIDE

LISBON

First Edition 2018

Editor: Sian Marsh
Author: Neil Schlecht, Abigail Blasi
Head of Production: Rebeka Davies
Picture Editor: Tom Smyth
Cartography Update: Carte
Update Production: Apa Digital
Photography Credits: AWL Images 1; Bigstock 24; Fotolia 68; iStock 4MC, 4ML, 5TC, 5MC, 18, 22, 70, 72; Lydia Evans/Apa Publications 4TC, 5T, 5MC, 5M, 6L, 6R, 7, 7R, 11, 13, 14, 17, 21, 26, 29, 30, 33, 34, 36, 39, 40, 41, 42, 45, 49, 50, 53, 54, 57, 60, 62, 64, 67, 74, 75, 76, 77, 78, 79, 80, 81, 82, 84, 85, 87, 89, 90, 92, 93, 94, 96, 99, 101, 103; Public domain 5M, 47, 58; Shutterstock 4TL, 35, 71
Cover Picture: iStock

Distribution
UK, Ireland and Europe: Apa Publications (UK) Ltd; sales@insightguides.com
United States and Canada: Ingram Publisher Services; ips@ingramcontent.com
Australia and New Zealand: Woodslane; info@woodslane.com.au
Southeast Asia: Apa Publications (SN) Pte; singaporeoffice@insightguides.com
Worldwide: Apa Publications (UK) Ltd; sales@insightguides.com

Special Sales, Content Licensing and CoPublishing
Insight Guides can be purchased in bulk quantities at discounted prices. We can create special editions, personalised jackets and corporate imprints tailored to your needs. sales@insightguides.com; www.insightguides.biz

Contact us
Every effort has been made to provide accurate information in this publication, but changes are inevitable. The publisher cannot be responsible for any resulting loss, inconvenience or injury. We would appreciate it if readers would call our attention to any errors or outdated information. We also welcome your suggestions; please contact us at: hello@insightguides.com
www.insightguides.com

Lisbon Metro

Odivelas
Senhor Roubado
Ameixoeira
Lumiar
Quinta das Conchas

Aeroporto
Encarnação
Moscavide
Oriente
Cabo Ruivo
Olivais
Chelas
Bela Vista
Olaias

Alfornelos
Pontinha
Amadora Este
Carnide
Telheiras
Campo Grande
Alvalade
Reboleira
Colégio Militar/Luz
Cidade Universitária
Roma
Alto dos Moinhos
Laranjeiras
Entre Campos
Jardim Zoológico
Campo Pequeno
Areeiro
Praça de Espanha
São Sebastião
Saldanha
Alameda
Parque
Picoas
Arroios (closed until 2019)
Anjos
Santa Apolónia
Rato
Marquês de Pombal
Intendente
Avenida
Martim Moniz
Restauradores
Rossio
Baixa-Chiado
Terreiro do Paço
Cais do Sodré

Blue Line
Yellow Line
Green Line
Red Line
O Interchange Station
o Station